Public Service Broadcasting

Key Concerns in Media Studies

Series editor: Andrew Crisell

Within the context of today's global, digital environment, *Key Concerns in Media Studies* addresses themes and concepts that are integral to the study of media. Concisely written by leading academics, the books consider the historical development of these themes and the theories that underpin them, and assess their overall significance, using up-to-date examples and case studies throughout. By giving a clear overview of each topic, the series provides an ideal starting point for all students of modern media.

Published

Paul Bowman   *Culture and the Media*

Andrew Crisell   *Liveness and Recording in the Media*

Tim Dwyer   *Legal and Ethical Issues in the Media*

Gerard Goggin   *New Technologies and the Media*

David Hendy   *Public Service Broadcasting*

Shaun Moores   *Media, Place and Mobility*

Forthcoming

Gerard Goggin and Kathleen Ellis   *Disability and the Media*

Niall Richardson and Sadie Wearing   *Gender and the Media*

Public Service Broadcasting

David Hendy

Professor of Media and Communications, University of Sussex

First published 2013 by
PALGRAVE MACMILLAN

Palgrave Macmillan in the UK is an imprint of Macmillan Publishers Limited,
registered in England, company number 785998, of Houndmills, Basingstoke,
Hampshire RG21 6XS.

Palgrave Macmillan in the US is a division of St Martin's Press LLC,
175 Fifth Avenue, New York, NY 10010.

Palgrave Macmillan is the global academic imprint of the above companies
and has companies and representatives throughout the world.

Palgrave® and Macmillan® are registered trademarks in the United States,
the United Kingdom, Europe and other countries.

ISBN: 978–0–230–23895–4

This book is printed on paper suitable for recycling and made from fully
managed and sustained forest sources. Logging, pulping and manufacturing
processes are expected to conform to the environmental regulations of the
country of origin.

A catalogue record for this book is available from the British Library.

A catalog record for this book is available from the Library of Congress.

10   9   8   7   6   5   4   3   2   1
22 21 20 19 18 17 16 15 14 13

Printed and bound in Great Britain by
CPI Antony Rowe, Chippenham and Eastbourne

To my parents,
Jim and Gaynor Hendy

Contents

Acknowledgements

This book has been written, in part, during research leave primarily devoted to other projects between 2009 and 2012. I would therefore like to acknowledge the generous support of: the Centre for Research in Arts, Social Sciences and Humanities at the University of Cambridge; the Leverhulme Trust; my former colleagues in the Communication and Media Research Institute at the University of Westminster; and my new colleagues in the School of Media, Film and Music at the University of Sussex. I also wish to thank those who have read earlier drafts, given me advice on various topics or prompted me to think more deeply about the purposes of broadcasting, including, in particular, Andrew Crisell, Jean Seaton, Anthony McNicholas, Hugh Chignell, Matt Thompson, Gwyneth Williams and Tony Ageh. References to archival material are by permission of the BBC Written Archives Centre, Caversham, and the Lilly Library, Indiana University-Bloomington. Finally, I would like to thank, as always, my wonderful family, for all their tolerance and support during the painfully drawn-out writing of this rather short book.

Introduction: Why Public Service Broadcasting?

You might expect a book on public service broadcasting to be nothing but a work of history. The whole concept, after all, has a certain last-century ring to it. It speaks of big corporations, nation-states, cultural elites, social engineering, top-down media. And, as the sociologist and ethnographer Georgina Born points out, each building block of the phrase – 'public', 'service' and 'broadcasting' – has long been cast into doubt (2005: 7). The notion of a collective 'public', for instance, has been undermined by an increasing discourse of individualism across the spectrum: from Margaret Thatcher's infamous declaration that there's 'no such thing as society' all the way to a radical belief in the emancipatory power of choice, diversity and self-expression. The concept of 'service' has at the same time come to seem a little patronising – as if people have been incapable of helping themselves and that there needed to be a cadre of people who, knowing better, can take decisions on their behalf. Then, finally, there's 'broadcasting'. With the rise of the Internet, television and radio have been recast as 'old' media. Not just old technologically, but ideologically redundant. A leading guru of the new 'Connected Age', Clay Shirky, now confidently dismisses our entire sixty years of television history as having been the equivalent of the eighteenth-century gin craze: something consumed to excess, driving us into a state of torpor, wasting vast chunks of our time. He even uses those worn-out phrases 'couch potatoes' and 'mindless' to conjure up a depressing vision of broadcasting's inherent, troubling passivity. For Shirky, 'Media in the twentieth century was run as a single event: consumption.' 'The animating question of media in that era', he suggests, 'was *If we produce more, will you consume more?*' (2010: 22).

If this was in fact the story of the twentieth century, we'd all surely be glad to have left it behind. But, fortunately, it is, at best, a half-truth. Which is why this book is indeed partly a work of history: one of its aims is to show the fatuity and condescension of such neophiliac claims by dealing with the past more accurately. It is telling, for instance, that

Shirky ignores radio, even though, having been around a lot longer and being more pervasive globally, it's accounted for many more hours of 'consumption' than television. He assumes, too, that what we've watched on screen is almost entirely beside the point. Quality has no part in his calculus. And he assumes that broadcasters have been motivated by nothing other than a desire to get us to 'consume more'. It seems to me that the reason for these absences is almost certainly because of another, deeper one: the absence of public service broadcasting from his purview. He writes from an American perspective. And in the United States there's been a much weaker public service broadcasting tradition. It exists – and, as David Goodman (2011) has shown, there's a whole lost dimension of civic-minded broadcasting to be rediscovered. But it's marginal. The United States, like many other countries of the world, has been dominated by a commercial model in which profit has undoubtedly been the key objective for those running the industry and in which, consequently, creativity and ambition have sometimes come a poor second. In many other parts of the world broadcasting's been run as an arm of the state, so that in dictatorships or imperfectly democratic countries in the former Soviet bloc, Asia and Africa, broadcasting's been a crudely handled and aesthetically impoverished tool of government. In these cases, though, we're dealing with a problem of economics or of politics. They say nothing about the true potential of broadcasting itself. And in many remaining parts of the world – in Western and Northern Europe, in India, Australia and New Zealand, and in Canada, for instance – a completely different model has long existed: broadcasting run neither by the state nor by private commercial interests, but by large public bodies working in what they have thought of as the public interest. Its distance from state or commercial systems is more than just rhetorical. Public service broadcasting has been profoundly different in its animating character. And its presence has helped ensure that television and radio – so often banal and disappointing – have equally often been marvellous, enjoyable, nourishing, richly creative, life-enhancing forces for many millions of people over many decades.

Even so, it might be said, that was *then* and this is *now*. Michael Tracey, who has charted what he calls the 'Decline and Fall' of public service broadcasting (1998), believes that if it was once the single most important social, cultural and journalistic phenomenon of the twentieth century, it had definitely become a corpse on leave by the start of the twenty-first. This book takes issue with that line. I accept that, in terms of popular consciousness, public service broadcasting probably reached something of a zenith in the middle of the last century. And I certainly accept that public service broadcasting has come under steadily increasing attack from both antipathetic governments and commercial rivals, both of which have a vested interest in weakening it. But we can't yet declare it dead. Indeed, there's a strong case to be made for saying that, despite all the assaults, it is thriving. It wins plenty of ratings battles. There also appears to be enduring popular support for its values and principles. In particular, the British Broadcasting Corporation (BBC) continues to be one of the dominant players in television, radio and many aspects of the new media – not just in Britain itself, but globally. Georgina Born suggests, rightly, that a long-established broadcaster such as the BBC needs to be 'renewed so as better to meet the demands of a diverse and increasingly fragmented society' (2005: 7). But in many respects that is exactly what it's been doing for years. One of the central themes of this book is that the core principles motivating it – and other public service broadcasters like it – have been continuously renewed and adapted. Sometimes, this has meant a dramatic change of direction. But very often, too, the process of renewal has been about recovering a sense of its original purposes. Perhaps the most important argument in this book, then, is that public service broadcasting is still, usually, animated by the same underlying principles upon which it was originally based. Its complex mix of continuity and change, I suggest, is more of an achievement than a problem.

In any case, this book is about the present and the future as much as it's about the past. That's because public service broadcasting matters *now* more acutely than ever. Although I think Tracey is far too pessimistic in declaring the age of public service broadcasting over, I agree that it's got fewer friends than at any time in its history. And I would certainly agree that its disappearance would represent a real and deep-seated crisis within liberal democracy. The value of a strong public dimension to media – free of commercial influence or political interference, universally accessible, pluralist in spirit, mindful of the value to be found in collective experiences and in nurturing our collective potential: this has, I believe, been magnified, not diminished, by the proliferation of new channels and new media. So this book is written with a sense of urgency. And although it discusses public service broadcasting's past in some detail, it does so in order to show that its ethical roots are robust enough and adaptable enough to be deployed in a wider defence of public media right now.

There are things this book is *not* about. For instance, though I have mentioned it several times already, it's not about the BBC as such. Public service broadcasting is something larger than that, and it manifests itself in many different forms around the world. Yet I haven't wanted to offer a global tour of all the public service broadcasters, noting every variant and trajectory. That would be to offer something a mile wide but only an inch thick. It also remains true that, as Born says, 'the BBC has a special place in the history and the imagining of public service broadcasting'. Because of this, she suggests, 'The BBC's fate, its capacity to reinvent public service broadcasting in testing conditions, is emblematic of the fate of the ideal itself' (2005: 7). In Britain, too, the BBC has profoundly influenced the shape of rival broadcasters, so that even the commercial system that has operated side by side with it has been shaped by similar core values. For Tracey that means, in his words, that Britain has had 'possibly the greatest single system of diverse, quality communication the world has ever seen' (1998: viii). I hope that where broadcasters such as the BBC have fallen short, I shall say as much in the pages that follow. Nevertheless, the claims made by Born and Tracey ring true overall. And the BBC is therefore inevitably a dominant feature of this present study. I hope that when I discuss the BBC at length, it really can be read as 'emblematic' of other experiences elsewhere. That, in any case is the spirit in which I have done so.

This book is also not about policy, or regulatory regimes, or funding, or technology, or even institutional structures. That is partly because plenty of good work has already been published on these aspects of public service broadcasting. In Britain, seminal texts have been written by, for example, Briggs (1995), Scannell and Cardiff (1991), Curran and Seaton (1997), Barnett and Curry (1994), Chignell (2011), O'Malley (1994) and others; in America, by Ledbetter (1997), Hilmes (1997) and now Goodman (2011); in Canada, by Vipond (1992); in Australia, by Inglis (1983), among others. There have already been several surveys of European media, which also offer a good roadmap of public service broadcasting's place in the contemporary media ecology (see Humphreys, 1996; d'Haenens *et al.*, 2011). There seemed little point in replicating all this work. This book's particular bias is also a result of my being a cultural historian. As such, I prefer to explore how public service broadcasting has expressed itself *in action* – through its programmes or in editorial debates or as part of daily life for the listeners and viewers for whom it's intended. But most of all, this book sets aside issues of policy and the rest because I believe that public service broadcasting, in the end, is deep down all about a set of *ideas* – and about an *ethos*. 'Ideology' would be too strong a word, making it sound too calculating and planned. But quality comes into it somewhere, probably – as does a whole raft of other values. All of these have emerged organically. So they can't be easily pinned down. As one former BBC Chairman said, it's 'no use trying to define good broadcasting' – one just 'recognized it' (Scannell, 2000: 1). Even so, certain themes help us create a rounded, if complex, picture of what we might agree as 'public service broadcasting' – and perhaps, while we are at it, 'good' broadcasting too. It is these themes that have therefore underpinned my own unfolding argument. They are, in turn: enlightenment, democracy, culture, service, choice and trust. These are 'values' espoused by public service broadcasters; they are also sites of contestation. But each forms the focus for one of the chapters that follow.

Chapter 1 is the most straightforwardly historical chapter, since it discusses the origins of broadcasting. However, it does not do so in institutional terms, nor even through examining the 'birth' of radio', but rather by exploring a widespread desire to radiate 'Enlightenment' ideals, especially in the immediate aftermath of the First World War. Chapter 2 is focused on the role of public service broadcasting in nurturing democracy. Though it does not aim to be a definitive survey of radio and television journalism across the last ninety years or so, its central concern is with news coverage, current affairs and topical debate. Chapter 3 tackles culture. The subject is potentially so immense that it can only be approached through a few selective examples, touching on the broad shift from Culture as an ideal to culture as a way of life, and, of course, the implications of multiculturalism. Chapter 4 shifts the focus to service. It does so by trying to get under the skin of producers – to see how they might conceive of their role and their relationship, as professionals, with members of the audience. The last two chapters are the least historical in flavour, focusing as they do on much more contemporary concerns. Chapter 5 examines the impact on public service broadcasting of competition, and the proliferation of channels that took off in the 1980s. But it does so by exploring the subject of choice, and, in the end, by questioning the validity of consumer sovereignty that underpins most critiques of the public sector. Chapter 6 focuses on new media, especially the Internet. But it does so by exploring the subject of trust. It argues for public service values being given a privileged place in the digital realm – indeed, that certain public service institutions might be best placed to hold this digital realm 'in trust' for future generations.

As will no doubt be clear, I am in favour of public service broadcasting. But that is not because of a sentimental desire for the comforts of a simpler past. Nor is it because of a love of tradition. It is because I believe in the human capacity to change – and to change for the better.

This also happens to be a belief inherent in the public service broadcasting mission. It does not seek to impose a static or monolithic conception of culture; it seeks to include us; it seeks to emancipate us. Naturally, it does not always succeed in all these goals. But as Tracey says, the arguments around public service broadcasting are always about so much more than broadcasting. They are 'about the whole character of our lives, about principles and values and moral systems' which prevail in the world at large (1998: xvi). So I hope the book as a whole makes a persuasive case: that the sheer *ambition* of public service broadcasting is not just a past achievement of which we can approve – it is also something which today, still, is too precious to throw away.

1 Enlightenment: First Principles, Deep Origins

Public service broadcasting had its formal, institutional birth in the early 1920s. But its sudden arrival in the years between the two world wars makes little sense unless we trace its deeper origins in the late nineteenth century and the years either side of the First World War. The individual men and women who went on to shape early broadcasting – people such as the Italian-born but British-based wireless entrepreneur Guglielmo Marconi, or the head of the Radio Corporation of America, David Sarnoff or the founding father of the BBC, John Reith – were all profoundly important. But their visions were shaped very much by larger social, cultural, political and technological forces. What, though, should our context be? How wide do we go? How far back in time do we glance?

Seaton, along with Briggs (1995), Scannell and Cardiff (1991), Crisell (2002) and Chignell (2011), in Britain, and others such as Douglas (1987) and Hilmes (1997) in America or Ross (2008) and Lacey (1996) in Germany, all point to the new conditions of mass culture, mass consumption and universal suffrage – all of which raised two pressing questions at the start of the 1920s: how to create an informed and cultured modern democracy; and how new kinds of mass media might help in that task. Current accounts also point to the rich tradition of Victorian paternalism that Reith's generation could draw upon: that middle-class desire to improve the less fortunate. Yet surprisingly few authors have pointed to the First World War as an important influence, or to the wider cultural and intellectual anxieties about moral and mental decline which seeped into Western consciousness during this period. One aim of this chapter, therefore, is to bring these 'neglected' themes back into focus.

There is another, deeper-rooted concept which also helps us to make sense of all these disparate factors: the idea of *Enlightenment* – the idea that first emerged in seventeenth-century Europe, and which asserted the radical notion that both coercive inequality and avoidable ignorance could be banished if rationality could prevail. This was a notion that placed education – the cultivation of a reasoning, deliberative approach to human affairs – centre-stage. In doing so, it recognized two things. First, human beings were all capable of *change*. Second, this being the case, society would be a better place if we collectively and individually attempted to fulfil this capacity by becoming more reasoning. This was not a complacent assumption that the world would steadily improve. Rather, 'it involved a sense of the possibility of constructing a future world that was different and thus the chance that it might be better' (Garnham, 2000: 5). It is this emancipatory project that was woven deeply into the fabric of public service broadcasting during its foundational years.

Private Wireless, Public Ether

If we take enlightenment to be one of our foundational principles, our first task is to expel Guglielmo Marconi from any narrative account of the origins of public service broadcasting. His is the name still most commonly associated with the 'invention' of radio – or 'wireless' as it was more commonly called in Britain – during the last years of the nineteenth century. Even on a strictly technical level, this reputation is largely undeserved. It was, after all, not Marconi but the British physicist Oliver Lodge who, in 1894, first publicly demonstrated the transmission of Morse code signals through the air by means of electromagnetic waves. Marconi's achievement over the years after 1896 was to collate or buy out the technical achievements of others such as Lodge, repackage them skilfully into marketable kits and then self-publicize his efforts (see Garratt, 2006; Lochte, 2000; Douglas, 1987; Crisell, 2002; Street, 2002). Nowhere did he think creatively about the new technology's wider dimension, let alone about it serving as a social *good*. His focus was on 'point-to-point' communication between a single sender and a single receiver – someone, say, on a ship in the middle of the Atlantic wishing to contact a relative back home in New York, a government official in Whitehall wishing to communicate with an overseas envoy in Africa, an army general behind the lines in Flanders wanting to send orders to his men up at the trenches. Conceptually, this was merely a refinement of private telegraphy or telephony. Both the sender and the receiver paid for the transaction. Or, if they didn't pay, they were certainly privileged participants in what we might call an early *ad hoc* 'subscription' service. The idea of signals freely radiating – signals broadcast across an entire region and thus potentially available to anyone – scared Marconi nearly out of his wits. His ambition was to establish, if possible, a global commercial monopoly in a 'closed' technology he claimed as his own. Between 1896 and the 1920s his role in radio was to suppress rival systems, try to drive competitors out of work and seek monopolistic deals with any government or military or commercial organization around the world – dubious or otherwise – which showed an interest in erecting new and more powerful chains of communication as a means of reinforcing control over land or people or goods (Headrick, 1992). It is instructive, for instance, to note that one of the Marconi Company's magazines, *Wireless World*, groaned heavily with the language of power during these formative years. It spoke of wireless as part of the 'arms race' or a 'branch of national service' – something that might protect or enhance a country's supremacy in the world. In short, what we might call 'Marconi-ism' promoted radio as a technology to supercharge the communicative efficacy of the state apparatus – and fill the coffers of a private company in the process (see Hendy, 2011, 2013).

This is worth highlighting because it represents so vividly the antithesis of public service broadcasting as it would come to be defined by the late 1920s. Quite unintentionally, however, Marconi-ism made two important contributions to foundational thinking about how the new technology of wireless might, despite everything, become a social good. First, the nakedly aggressive nature of Marconi's business enterprise provided an early warning of the dangers in one company achieving a commercial monopoly. Before the First World War, for example, the British government started lengthy negotiations with the Company over the building of an Imperial Wireless Chain of stations linking Britain with Egypt, Aden, India and South Africa. Marconi consistently sought to crush any rival bidders and secure exclusive contracts. In America, the federal government's response was simply to create a rival private monopoly of its own – one that was at least fully 'American': the Radio Corporation of America, incorporated in 1919. British politicians dithered. But by the 1920s the political climate was broadly moving in favour of something closer to state control. The 1914–18 war had offered important lessons. With its heightened need for speedy communications in battle, the flood of wireless propaganda hurled into the airwaves seeking to influence newspaper reporting on both sides and its whipped-up anxiety over spying or the threat of invasions led by hundreds of radio-controlled aircraft, the war had everywhere intensified a feeling among politicians that wireless was a technology of national importance that should somehow be placed under national direction. Indeed, four years of war had demonstrated the effectiveness in general of centralized administrative control of utilities such as health, coal and food, in harnessing national resources.

By the opening of the 1920s, then, two rather different agendas reinforced each other. One was the 'military-industrial' urge to ensure tight central control of powerful technology. The other was a strengthening faith in the ability of experts and civil servants – the rising professional classes – to run affairs more effectively than market forces or the gentlemen-amateurs of the political elites (Curran and Seaton, 1997: 113–15). The former preferred some form of direct state control; the latter could point to the success of arm's-length 'public corporations' such as those running forestry, water or electricity – bodies acting in the national interest but at one remove from the state.

The second of Marconi's entirely unintended contributions to ensuring radio had a future as a social good rather than as a private scheme of enrichment was to stimulate interest in listening to wireless among hundreds – and, eventually, thousands – of ordinary people. These were the 'wireless amateurs' who sprang up on both sides of the Atlantic between the first decade of the twentieth century and the early 1920s: individuals who had realized that, whatever the commercial or military operators had envisaged about the privacy of their messages, signals radiated freely through the air, and could be hauled in from the electro-magnetic realm by whoever was motivated enough to build simple receiving equipment in their homes or garden sheds.

This was, albeit briefly, a thriving subculture. By 1912, the *New York Times* estimated there were 'several hundred thousand' such operators in the United States (Douglas, 1987: 198). In Britain there were only a few hundred transmitting, but several thousand more were equipped to receive. One estimate of the number of amateur enthusiasts in pre-war Germany was 100,000 (Gilfillan, 2009: 36). The wireless scene was described as a craze; by 1918, like influenza, it was being likened to a pandemic.

Before war temporarily shut down all this activity, it established important possibilities for the future. Most obviously, an unforeseen but potentially huge public audience for wireless had been conceived – as had a market for the sale of homemade wireless 'kits'. This raised the prospect of transmissions that were not just overheard by the public but actually made especially for them. It also showed that wireless could be thought of not just as a weapon or a revenue tool but as a source of domestic pleasure. As Douglas suggests, the wireless companies had unleashed forces they were struggling to control. Very quickly, in fact, 'the concepts of corporate monopoly or military pre-emption seemed alien, mean-spirited, and completely unenforceable' (1987: 194).

It is tempting to see in the amateur wireless boom a prototype of public broadcasting that was truly democratic and participatory – a fragile, creative flowering that would be horribly crushed by the big 'top-down' corporations and networks that emerged in the 1920s. And indeed several writers have suggested that these 'early sparks' carved out a 'space of experimental possibility' (Squier, 2003: 6–35; Gilfillan, 2009: 36). We can even point to some striking parallels with our own century's 'Web 2.0' revolution. Rather like today's Internet users – not just *consuming* the distributed media products of big broadcasting organizations, but busy *creating* online blogs, uploading 'homemade' videos or nurturing our own social communities on Facebook – the early wireless amateurs were apparently resisting regulation or censorship and creating an exciting electronic free-for-all without hierarchy or centre. This, though, relies on a largely mythical version of broadcasting's origins. Wireless, with its mysterious signals and voices travelling unseen through the air, undoubtedly captured the public imagination well before organized broadcasting appeared. But the creative and ethical vision of most amateur enthusiasts was strictly limited. They distinguished fiercely, for example, between 'irresponsible' amateurs and 'genuine' experimenters. The former, those who broadcast anything that took their fancy or who maybe took pleasure in hearing such material for its own sake, needed to be disciplined or perhaps excluded from the airwaves altogether. The proper role of the amateur was *not* to listen or enjoy: it was to pursue the manly task of perfecting technology through a laborious process of test transmissions. What exactly such technology was ultimately for scarcely mattered. This was 'participatory' media, to be sure. But it had a distinctly authoritarian and narrow-minded edge (Hendy, 2013).

In the end the wireless amateur's efforts to 'own' this new technology proved irrelevant. For just as Marconi had failed to restrict radio to a means of private point-to-point communication, the amateurs, in turn, were unable to suppress the intrinsically democratic nature of their own transmissions. A larger audience had been created, and it could not be un-created. Moreover, what made wireless so magical – so powerful – was precisely that it was, in principle, accessible to all. The key to this notion of accessibility was the ether itself, a centuries-old concept of a mysterious, all-encompassing but invisible medium that pervaded all things – that became, in effect, a 'connecting medium' binding together and making coherent what would otherwise be a chaos of individual elements. That its actual existence was now being disproved by Einstein's new physics of relativity scarcely mattered. It somehow suggested the underlying unity of human existence. This, in turn, linked the new technology with some of the most utopian thinking of the age. Here, by implication, was an infinitely extendable, shareable resource, a medium for spreading ideas far and wide, for transcending physical and political barriers, for uniting the hitherto disunited. After the carnage of the First World War, it was the kind of resource that seemed more necessary than ever.

This, no doubt, was why, at the League of Nations' first assembly in Geneva during November 1920, a small *ad hoc* wireless station was set up. The man running it, Arthur Burrows, had managed a news service during the war and experienced just enough of the frontline to become a lifelong pacifist. 'Wireless', he said soon afterwards, now had a purpose: to be a tool for *dis*armament, to 'alter for the better the social life of the people and international relations', to 'assist the progress of civilization', to provide a platform open to a variety of views but, above all, to 'spread throughout the world a doctrine of common sense' (BBC WAC, 1923). Similarly, in a new magazine which first appears in 1922, the *Broadcaster*, we start to find articles extolling radio's ability to 'make for the gaiety of nations and introduce a humanizing note when scattered peoples are brought into closer contact' (*Broadcaster*, August and September 1922). So a profound shift had taken place by the early 1920s. Radio had evolved from its conceptual birth in the 1890s as a tool for private, linear communication into something freely radiated and bracingly public. Just as important, there were people who'd found for it an *ethical* purpose. Utopian ideas once attached to the nineteenth century's ether had been bequeathed to the modern 'electromagnetic spectrum'. This spectrum – which, in most people's minds, was identical to the very air in which it operated – felt as if it were public property. As such, it wasn't just a shareable resource: it also created a collective sensibility, or what in 1935 two American social psychologists would call a 'consciousness of kind' (Cantril and Allport, 1935: 18).

In 1920, the question of *how* precisely this 'consciousness of kind' might be harnessed was yet to be settled. The libertarian rhetoric of the wireless amateurs still argued for an ether populated by thousands of 'micro'-broadcasters. They assumed ordinary people would be as interested in transmitting as in receiving, and that the content was almost incidental. But, as Arthur Burrows and the *Broadcaster* magazine showed, there were plenty of people at ease with the notion that, while the ether itself had no centre and no hierarchy, broadcasting could be something done *by others for us*: that it might become, very consciously, a meaningful, substantive *one-way* communicative act – a gift, as it were, offered to all, with no demand for reciprocation and with the hope that in the process ordinary life might be made more interesting, more peaceful and more pleasurable.

Mass Culture and the Public Mind

The idea of broadcasting as a tool for improving modern life was, by itself, rather vague. What gave it coherence – indeed, a sense of urgency – was an anxiety among the upper middle and professional classes of the late nineteenth and early twentieth century over the apparently sudden rise of 'mass' society, or, more specifically, 'mass' *culture*. Since the 1880s, industrialization across the Western world had created a growing working-class population. Poverty remained widespread. But wages were rising, and even a modest surplus income within each family, once aggregated, created a market for goods and services sizeable enough to be worth cultivating. A lower middle class of clerks, salespeople and shop assistants was also expanding fast. For both groups, too, there was more free time: Saturdays and Bank Holidays off, labour-saving devices on sale everywhere, an organized leisure industry of seaside holidays, spectator sports, popular newspapers, cheap books, department stores, music halls and cinemas (Searle, 2004: 107–15, 530–70). For those privileged few who had long had access to art and leisure, the key question was this: did such cultural democratization mean progress – or did more mean worse?

Their worry was not so much with popular taste: after all, that had always been dismissed as vulgar. It was with 'mass culture' – the moderately aspirational tastes of a newly literate public 'craving instruction and entertainment more than cultivation' (Gildea, 2008: 390–1). This was a public that might, for example, enjoy a little light classical music, or buy cheap reprints of the classics. Yet culture wasn't supposed to be mass produced like this. It was supposed to be elevated, rare, noble, pure, exquisite, enduring, moral, transcendent – in short, something for the few, since, of course, only the few were deemed capable of appreciating these qualities. For someone such as George Gissing, the author of *New Grub Street* (1891), culture was being sullied – dragged down into a branch of trade by the demands of the 'quarter-educated' (Searle, 2004: 572).

The response to this imagined degradation generally took one of two forms. The first, for those with most contempt for the masses, was to erect new barriers between their own versions of culture and those they saw as crassly commercial and dangerously standardized. They embraced and promoted the avant-garde: dissonant music, non-realist novels, abstract paintings. This was 'coterie art with a vengeance', and the more difficult it was to appreciate, the better (Searle, 2004: 577; Carey, 1992). The second response came from those who believed that the masses – though usually showing regrettable taste – were at least capable of refinement. They believed mass culture shouldn't be ignored: it should be improved. This passion for bettering the lot of those below had deep roots. It contained a mix of Christian charity, middle-class altruism and nineteenth-century socialism. And in its various forms it was precisely this second response – this idea of *service* – which was later 'grafted onto broadcasting in its formative period' (Scannell, 2000: 55).

Historians have pointed to one articulation of this Victorian-era paternalism more than any other, because of the profound influence it had on cultural debates for years to come – in Britain, at least: Matthew Arnold's 1869 essay, *Culture and Anarchy*. This short book, reprinted many times over, combined a fairly traditional interpretation of culture with a more radical proposal for its direction and use. Like many of his contemporaries Arnold was worried by the mob, convinced it was never more than a hair's breadth away from open revolt. But he detected a wider crisis. There was, he said, a self-indulgent tendency among all classes to do as one pleased: to *do* rather than to *think*; to be what one *was* rather than to strive to be *better*. The toiling masses – 'raw and half-developed' – could hardly help themselves (Arnold, 1875: 94). Yet the aristocracy were just as busy indulging their own pleasures, while the middle classes and the 'rising' working class were 'Philistines': stiff-necked, lacking curiosity, self-satisfied. Anarchy beckoned – or, in the ruling classes' overreaction to the threat of anarchy, autocracy. A road to salvation, however, lay with culture. Arnold defined this, not as something which belonged to the elite, nor as 'a mere thing for its own sake'. Culture was 'the study of perfection', a pursuit of wisdom and beauty – or, as Arnold liked to put it, of 'sweetness and light' (15–16, 20–1). Anyone engaged in this pursuit would transcend their base instincts and find their 'best self' (6, 80–1). In this way, culture would incorporate the working classes 'within the existing social and political order' and so alleviate 'the strain and hostility between the classes in a deeply divided society' (Scannell, 2000: 56).

Beyond this general thesis, three other aspects of *Culture and Anarchy* are worth highlighting here. They're often overlooked; but they're crucial to understanding Arnold's relevance to later thinking about public broadcasting.

First, his vision of what constituted culture, though in many ways shaped by the prejudices of his class, was neither unbending nor narrow. The 'essence of an epoch', he declared, 'is a movement of ideas': nothing should remain fixed, since 'making a stream of fresh thought play freely from our stock notions and habits, is what is most wanted by us at present' (Arnold, 1875: 65, 174). For Arnold, as Raymond Williams pointed out, culture was not merely literary; nor was it only about rational thinking. It involved cultivating 'all sides of our humanity' (1987: 115). Spreading culture was therefore an ongoing task. The pursuit of 'light and perfection', he wrote, consisted 'not in resting and being, but in growing and becoming, in a perpetual advance' (Arnold, 1875: 73).

Second, Arnold did not just call for *individuals* to improve themselves through culture. Indeed it was precisely individualism that led people into indulgently following their 'base instincts' instead of embracing a spirit of generosity toward others. Instead, Arnold promoted 'the noble aspiration to leave the world better and happier than we found it' (7–8). 'The expansion of our humanity', he explained, must therefore be 'a general expansion'. To avoid being stunted, a person had to 'carry others along' in this march towards perfection, 'continually doing all he can to enlarge and increase the volume of the human stream sweeping thitherward' (12). Culture, in other words, wasn't simply about sweetness and light. It was about making sweetness and light prevail:

> it knows that the sweetness and light of the few must be imperfect until the raw and unkindled masses of humanity are touched by sweetness and light ... we must have a broad basis, must have sweetness and light for as many as possible ... . Those are the happy moments of humanity... when there is a national glow of life and thought, when the whole of society is in the fullest measure permeated by thought, sensible to beauty, intelligent and alive. Only it must be *real* thought and *real* beauty, *real* sweetness and *real* light. Plenty of people will try to give the masses, as they call them, an ineffectual food prepared and adapted in the way they think proper for the actual condition of the masses ... . Plenty of people will try to indoctrinate the masses with the set of ideas and judgments constituting the creed of their own profession or party ... but culture works differently. It does not try to teach down to the level of inferior classes; it does not try to win them for this or that sect of its own,

with ready-made judgments and watch-words. It seeks to do away with classes; to make the best that has been thought and known in the world current everywhere; to make all men live in an atmosphere of sweetness and light, where they may use ideas, as it uses them itself, freely, – nourished, and not bound by them ... . This is the social idea; and the men of culture are the true apostles of equality.

(43–4)

This passage is worth quoting at length because it anticipates beautifully many of the core ideas that later emerged within the BBC and, in particular, many of the core ideas in what will eventually be called Reithianism. It was a vigorous, all-encompassing assertion of the power of culture to nourish and educate all.

The third key idea woven through Arnold's essay follows logically from the second. If sectional interests were to be avoided – and they clearly needed to be, for they were invariably self-serving – then the massive task of collective betterment needed to be co-ordinated by an institution or body which somehow transcended any particular party, profession or creed. For Arnold, it was only the state that could do this. This did not mean the 'governing classes': they were a pretty ineffective lot, made up as they were of Barbarians and Philistines. Instead, there needed to be a new 'organ of our collective best self, of our national right reason' – something that could harness 'the fermenting mind of the nation'. This had to be formed from individuals who would leave their class – and their class prejudices – behind: people led by 'a general *humane* spirit', who had already found their 'best self' and might therefore be able to awaken the best self latent in everyone else (Arnold, 1875: 83, 100; Williams, 1987: 121–2).

Writing in 1958, Raymond Williams pointed out how priggish the tone of *Culture and Anarchy* seems to modern minds. Yet he doubted that 'any quick and ready alternative for the achievement of Arnold's ends has in fact, in the ninety years since he wrote, manifested itself' (122). Certainly, in the aftermath of the First World War, many of the issues Arnold had identified in the 1860s seemed more pressing than ever. The mechanized slaughter of war had prompted a gloomy prognosis among many intellectuals: that humanity was a lost cause and Western civilization in crisis – a prognosis that won big audiences in a population 'receptive to anxiety' (Overy, 2009: 2). In America, less directly affected by the ravages of war but facing the wrenching disruptions of rapid industrialization, urbanization and mass immigration, cultural commentators worried about the ability of a new and highly individualistic country to assimilate peacefully and equitably. Britain was awash with pamphlets and books and public lectures talking of economic or political or moral decline – even of biological decline, mental decline. The Victorians had at least imagined a world of inevitable progress. But the post-war generation saw reason and hope ebbing away. One factor in this was the intimate experience of war for hundreds of thousands of young men: hitherto unimagined degrees of squalor and misery in the trenches prompting a disquieting sense of disillusionment and futility (Fussell, 2000: 3, 35). A second factor was a widespread anxiety over the psychological stability of the public at large. Very few Britons in 1920 would have read for themselves Sigmund Freud's ideas on the unconscious. Nevertheless, as Mathew Thomson has shown, a bastardized brew of Freudian ideas, contained in books such as *The Interpretation of Dreams* or *The Ego and the Id*, percolated 'into the culture, the social fabric, and the mentality of the era' through pop-psychology manuals and magazine advice columns (Thomson, 2001: 104). Similar interest in the 'savage within' could be found among anthropologists, economists and novelists. Many concerned people would therefore have agreed, if rather vaguely, with a key precept of psychoanalysis: that concealed beneath one's rather fragile conscious mind there seethed in the *un*conscious a chaos of primitive instincts ready to erupt at any moment. Instability was – or at least, was *felt* to be – everywhere.

If people's thoughts and opinions were understood as malleable, it surely suggested that people were also highly suggestible. And if they were suggestible, they would also, surely, be vulnerable to the simplistic but mesmerising charms of cheap and easy culture, jingoism and demagoguery. This would not have mattered but for the fact that the post-war period had also ushered in the era of universal suffrage. Since nearly everyone now had the vote, people's mental ability – their level of education and particularly their capacity to sift through information and process it rationally – had suddenly become a real political problem.

Modern democracy, then, revealed in stark terms the need for a rapid improvement in public education. Yet existing structures of learning were wholly inadequate to the task. Universities were for the most privileged of minorities. Even basic schooling was far from universal. As for the Church's influence, that was waning thanks to increasing secularization (Garnham, 2000: 10). For many influential thinkers, the best – perhaps the only – hope of creating 'organized intelligence' lay with new forms of mass communication (Czitrom, 1982: 102). Indeed, for someone such as the American philosopher

John Dewey, mass communication was *the* defining aspect of modern life. In his 1915 book, *Democracy and Education*, for instance, he argued that:

> Society not only continues to exist by transmission, by communication, but it may fairly be said to exist in transmission, in communication … . Men live in a community in virtue of the things they have in common; and communication is the way in which they come to possess things in common.
>
> (in Czitrom, 1982: 108)

But which means of mass communication might best allow humanity to 'possess things in common'? The press seemed ill prepared. In Britain, the early decades of the new century saw a flowering of weekly magazines such as *New Age* or the *Nation*, each featuring plenty of lively debate about literature and culture and politics. But while they busily discussed how their writers should give 'light and leading to their fellow citizens', it was hard to see how they could have an impact with sales of a mere 4,000 copies or so. True, there were now easily affordable mass-circulation newspapers. By 1900, the *Daily Mail* reached a million British breakfast tables every day (Searle, 2004: 111). But such newspapers were too often the private fiefdoms of their owners. They tended to reflect their prejudices and business interests rather than function as vehicles for the free exchange of ideas. Moreover, the drive to increase circulations and thus profits meant that, far from creating 'organized intelligence', papers regularly published the kind of lurid stuff that was likely to *de*stabilize public opinion. A reputation for sensational reporting was cemented in the public mind in the course of the First World War, when an endless stream of atrocity stories and invasion scares was later followed by the revelation that they had been largely fictional. This, Fussell argued, created a post-war generation with a 'lifelong suspicion of the press' (Fussell, 2000: 316). Even if the propagandist output of the wartime papers has been exaggerated, as more recent work by Adrian Gregory suggests, it remains the case that many editors did little to actively challenge the popular folktales and urban myths that swirled through the country, simply because being 'beastly to the Hun was good business' while 'fair-mindedness might be ruinous' (2008: 40–69). Perhaps the biggest obstacle to newspapers satisfying Dewey's ideal of knowledge held in common, however, was simply that they were so highly segmented by class. Dailies such as *The Times* had an almost exclusively upper-middle-class readership; the *Daily Mail* was read by the lower middle classes; most working-class families made do with Sunday papers. There was little shared experience.

By the 1920s, however, there was radio: a form of communication that suddenly seemed tailor-made for achieving the mass enlightenment that exercised Dewey and the 'sweetness and light' Matthew Arnold had sought half a century before. In principle, it could reach into every home, indifferent to class or reading ability. Its possibilities gradually dawned on a generation of thinkers, public administrators and entrepreneurs across the developed world. In America, a young employee of the Marconi Company, David Sarnoff, urged his managers to think of radio as a 'household utility', simple to operate and providing for those living far away from the cultural attractions of the city a chance to enjoy 'concerts, lectures, music recitals, etc.' in the comfort of their own home (Crisell, 2002: 12). In the Soviet Union in 1921 the Russian artist Velimir Khlebnikov conjured up a prophetic vision of a technological future in which, through radio, daily news and weather reports, lectures and advice would fly out of a central station 'like the flight of birds in springtime' to be heard in 'Radioauditoriums' built in every town. Into radio's hands 'the organization of popular education will pass', he predicted (1985: 155–9). In Britain, a less high-flown, though ultimately more successful version could be found in the words of Arthur Burrows, drawing on his direct experience at the League of Nations. Radio, Burrows announced, was bound to be educational. It would be so simply because 'the desire to interest all sections of the community' would tend to produce broadcasting material that was non-partisan and hence 'keeps us of open mind' (BBC WAC, 1923). Although the rapid spread of radio in the early 1920s across both Europe and America would fail to create a system of broadcasting that could ever live up to such utopian hopes, a mixed output of speech and music for the enjoyment and education of whoever was within reach of the signal was soon on offer. In short, radio was being offered as – and seen to be – an irredeemably *public* phenomenon.

It was in Britain, however, that the most overtly public-orientated broadcasting service appeared in the form of the British Broadcasting Company. Government officials had been anxious to avoid what they regarded as the American experience of 'chaos in the ether'; but politicians also had no interest in broadcasting being done directly by the state and were equally wary of allowing a company such as Marconi to achieve a commercial monopoly. The solution was to allow the various manufacturers to combine, which they did in October 1922. The new British Broadcasting Company was not, strictly speaking, a monopoly:

any bona fide manufacturer of radio sets in Britain could join. Nor, despite the Postmaster-General's professed hope that 'if the ether was to be occupied' it should be 'worthily occupied', was there yet a clearly stated ethical goal for the organization. Its stations were simply to provide 'news, information, concerts, lectures, educational matter, speeches, weather reports, theatrical entertainment and any other matter which for the time being may be permitted' (Briggs, 1995, v.1: 116).

For many involved this solid, somewhat uninspiring recipe would be enough to attract an audience – and thus a profit – without causing unnecessary fuss. Yet, the licence from the Post Office also instructed the Company to 'develop and exploit the said service' (116). There was no prescription as to what, in practical terms, this might mean. But, as it turned out, the edict was sufficiently open for key figures involved to seize their opportunity – to make the new organization into something bigger, more ambitious and much more influential than hitherto imagined. One of those figures in 1922 was Arthur Burrows. Not only was his the first voice on the British Broadcasting Company's airwaves in November 1922. He also became its first Director of Programmes and brought to that role all his previous thinking as to what broadcasting might become. Burrows, however, was only one of several 'founding fathers'. Another, who arrived at the BBC in 1922 without Burrow's direct experience of radio and without his clear idea of its potential, was a young Scotsman, John Reith. Within a few years it was Reith who led the Company into becoming the British Broadcasting *Corporation*, first as its General Manager, then as its first Director-General. It was therefore Reith who, more than any other single figure, helped turn the BBC within less than a decade into the most famous public service broadcasting organization in the world.

Reithianism

It has sometimes been assumed that the BBC was essentially the singular achievement of Reith. He certainly gave it 'form and purpose' (Briggs, 1995, v.1: 127). Here was a megalomaniac who was 'pompous, humourless, arrogant', Seaton suggests. But 'the near absurdity of his vision enabled him to foresee the power of the new service' (Curran and Seaton, 1997: 111–12). The vision, then, is to some extent inseparable from the man. Unfortunately, the man is also often inseparable from a stereotype. We know he was dominating and steeped in a rather rigid

Presbyterian morality. He could be boneheaded, regarding large swathes of modern art and modern literature as 'weird and repugnant' (McIntyre, 1993: 94). Yet there is another Reith, typically occluded: a man surprisingly tolerant of those he thought talented, and loyal to those he thought loyal to him. He even recognized his own psychological weaknesses: he read the scriptures; but he also read Freud. Beneath the bluster lurked a complex man. To start understanding Reithianism, we have to understand Reith himself.

There is, for instance, the profound influence of the war. We can trace Reith's autocratic style from his experience in 1917 co-ordinating arms supplies in a Philadelphia factory: it was there that he picked up the industrialist's ruthless concern for efficiency and distrust of organized labour (10, 63). He had also been in the trenches, where he found himself infused with a sense of righteousness. In his memoirs he recalled becoming, as a transport officer, 'conscious of powers of leadership in myself' (Reith, 1924: 31). After the war only his ultimate goal was clear: 'I wanted to use to the maximum effect the gifts I had and to do the greatest good I could' he declared (1924: 150). When he joined the embryonic BBC in 1922 he clearly retained an insatiate desire to offer someone or some*thing* his own brand of strong-willed, moralistic leadership. This blatant thirst for power is unappealing to modern tastes. For the American historian Todd Avery, for instance, his reputation as a 'Mussolini figure' is entirely apt. Avery even suggests Reith harboured sympathy 'for a totalitarian usage of radio such as would soon occur in Hitler's Germany' (Avery, 2006: 7). Yet, it's important to remember the pervasive anxiety about social unrest and mental decline in 1920s Britain. What accompanied this was a widely shared desire for strong men and drastic action. As one 1932 profile of Reith pointed out, 'He is the type of "hero" – dictator, if you will – that the time is throwing up in answer to an abysmal need' (McIntyre, 1993: 87). If he was forbidding and dominating, then, there were plenty of people willing to fall in behind him. This was especially the case when Reith started to develop a vision of broadcasting as a social tool in the tradition of Matthew Arnold. Drawing on this ethical tradition was, as Avery so neatly puts it, the 'galvanic spark' that brought radio to social and cultural life in Britain (2006: 7). For what Reith found in broadcasting was a practical and powerful means of applying Arnold's earlier cultural prescription.

Reith's grand manifesto was his 1924 book, *Broadcast over Britain* – a key text in the history of public broadcasting. In it, Reith suggests that broadcasting is an *undemocratic* tool for achieving highly *democratic* purposes. This emerges throughout the book in three ways. First, there is an argument related to inclusivity. In the past, Reith points out, 'a very large proportion of the people were shut off from first-hand knowledge of the events which make history'. But radio, being broadcast 'for any and all to receive', allows everyone – not just those 'with Fortune's twin-keys: Leisure and Money' – to 'gain access' to the world of politics and culture (1924: 15–17). It is something that 'may be shared by all alike, for the same outlay, and to the same extent':

> The genius and the fool, the wealthy and the poor listen simultaneously, and to the same event, and the satisfaction of the one may be as great as that of the other … . There need be no first and third class.
> (217–18)

This lack of exclusivity means that 'Great men' and great ideas – the 'sweetness and light' of Arnold's dream – are able to reach parts of the nation hitherto overlooked. The electorate as a whole will be 'more intelligent and enlightened' (113). Indeed, it's vital that broadcasting doesn't just make available 'the best in every department in human knowledge, endeavour and achievement' to those who want it: 'our responsibility', Reith points out, is to carry it 'into the greatest possible number of homes' – to keep in view 'the maximum benefit to the maximum number' (34, 64). To put it in Arnold's terms, it is emphatically not about cultivating *ourselves*; it is about what we can provide for *everyone*, about making culture and wisdom *prevail*.

A second strand of Reith's argument is that this attempt to 'uplift' culture has to be dynamic. To give people what they already want is merely to keep culture, knowledge or levels of education, static. In any case, Reith says, while most people do not know what they need, they also often do not even know what they want, since to want something they have to know it exists, or at least be able to conceive of it. Hence the broadcaster's mission must be to introduce people to new and unfamiliar things: art, literature, ideas, music or arguments that they won't necessarily have come across. Only then can people even begin to choose wisely. In doing this the broadcaster needs to 'set the pace' because, as Reith famously emphasizes, 'The more one gets, the more one wants' (27). In other words, he calls for a complete inversion of the market model in which supply follows demand. For broadcasting to be a service – that is, for it to leave the world a better place – it has to ensure that demand *follows* supply. This, however, is not a case of handing down culture from on high without a thought for how it's received. The broadcaster has to be constantly imaginative if output isn't to stagnate and become predictable and so lose its value, or indeed its audience. As Reith puts it, programmes have to 'go with a swing', for no sweetness and light can prevail unless large numbers of people are listening in the first place. Popularity and style – not just content – are therefore entirely legitimate concerns for the public service broadcaster.

The third strand of Reith's argument follows from the other two – namely that the range of programmes on offer has to be broad and diverse. This isn't just because of that 'maximum benefit to the maximum number' argument, important though that is to Reith's vision. It is also because broadcasting must 'appeal to every kind of home' (78). Anyone reading Reith's own words here for the first time might be shocked, since his emphasis on 'everything that is best' has slowly solidified into a contemporary belief that he only wanted to broadcast rigorously uplifting works of high culture. Yet take this important – but often overlooked – passage in his book:

> I do not in any way imply that merit is to be found exclusively in the classics of music or literature, or that transmissions of this nature are the only ones in which the broadcaster is really interested or the only ones which he feels are worth doing. If this were his view ... it would indicate an entire misconception of his function. It is most important that light and 'entertaining' items be sent out. The broadcaster puts as much energy and care into work of this nature, which shall constitute a pleasing relaxation after a hard day's work, as into items which tend to edification and wider knowledge.
>
> (133–4)

Obviously, this falls well short of unbridled populism. Entertainment is here conceived as a reward for good behaviour rather than something embraced for its own sake. Yet the passage shows Reith conceiving of broadcasting as needing to cater to people's whole identity: to their need for pleasure as well as work, their need for fiction as well as fact, their need for calm as well as excitement – their need, in short, to be happy, rounded beings, rather than merely coldly rational and efficient ones. Furthermore, in other passages the book pleads for a certain amount of tolerance. Reith recognizes, for instance, that 'one man's meat is another's poison' (120). 'The common denominator of a nation is not so easily determined', he says, 'and in any event it keeps changing.' Even if it could be found, 'individual peculiarities have to be catered for to some extent also'. Indeed, he argues, 'It benefits us – makes us more charitable – to know and understand that others have different tastes and ideas' (123–4). Like Arnold's before him, Reith's conception of human nature – and how it might be changed – was more open than the popular image might suggest. His paternalism may have little appeal to contemporary tastes. But it should not be interpreted as crudely reactionary – nor, indeed, as strikingly out of tune with the thinking of his own time. When Reith argued, in effect, that good culture need only be made available for most people to embrace it, he was showing a typical 'rationalist faith in the liberating potential of great ideas' (LeMahieu, 1988: 146).

Against the background of these three intertwined arguments, other components of the 'Reithian' philosophy of public service broadcasting begin to make more sense. Let me offer just offer two examples. First, a very specific one: Reith's infamous insistence on the use of 'received pronunciation' – that is, the accent and style of southern 'educated' English – by all the BBC's announcers. Clearly, at one level, it was a narrow-minded policy, utterly blind to the legitimacy of regional accents. But the aim, Reith explained, was to provide a model that anyone and everyone could emulate, so that no-one would have to 'go through life handicapped by the mistakes or carelessness of his own mispronunciation' (Reith, 1924: 161). Standardized pronunciation he viewed as an equalizing force (see Hendy, 2006). The second example is broader: Reith's insistence on the BBC having a monopoly of broadcasting in Britain. The very term 'monopoly' is anathema to us today, enjoying as we do an era of apparently unlimited choice. But, again, Reith's reasoning is that what he calls 'unity of control' allows for the efficient spread of good practice: high standards are promulgated everywhere, available to everyone, not just a few. He wrote menacingly of the 'brute force' of monopoly. But, as LeMahieu argues, this was merely an expression of his Manichean worldview, whereby his natural response to those forces ranged against him was simply to insist 'that the countervailing forces be made as strong' (1988: 143).

Was Reith guilty of forcing upon the British people his own, highly idiosyncratic vision of broadcasting? Clearly, he never doubted that he himself knew what was in other people's interest rather better than they did themselves. But this paternalist philosophy was really just a vigorously expressed version of a more widely held attitude: a popular interest in improving oneself, combined with a willingness to seek guidance from above as to how this might be achieved (Rose, 2001). The BBC also 'gained the consent of key brokers in British society' for his vision (LeMahieu, 1988: 148). Wireless manufacturers were happy to share the proceeds of an expanding market; the press decided it was easier to deal with a regulated monopoly than a series of direct competitors when it came to the supply of news; and when it came to political endorsement of the monopoly in 1925, Parliament didn't demur, either: Conservatives liked authority, Labour disliked private enterprise (McIntyre, 1993: 140). Finally, and perhaps decisively, Reith's paternalism could never be imposed through coercion, simply because the BBC couldn't force people to turn on their radio sets or to keep listening attentively when they did. To maintain its power, the BBC needed to persuade people to trust it as an honest and friendly guide; it needed people to like its output enough to turn on their sets day-in day-out.

A more enduring philosophical argument against Reithianism is that it embodied a broader – more disturbing – aspect of modernity: playing its part in the steady construction of what's been called the 'iron cage' of rationality. The notion, first articulated by Max Weber in the 1920s, but influential among several generations of theorists ever since – especially Michel Foucault and various post-modernists in the 1960s and 1970s – is essentially that the increasingly secular and technocratic character of life involved imposing far too much order and rational thinking on a complex world. This made the world efficient. But it also made it increasingly disciplinarian – a world with progressively less room for enchantment, individuality, serendipity, freedom. So, as Michael Bailey argues, the BBC might be understood as one of the 'cultural technologies' of government – that is, as a tool for governing conduct as much as for reforming lives (2007: 96–108). There *is* a countervailing argument, however. As Garnham points out, while a Foucauldian might see the 'discipline' dispensed through broadcasting as an alienating exercise of power, a writer such as Norbert Elias would have seen it as 'a civilizing process' (2000: 37). Enlightenment principles were always about finding an elusive but worthwhile balance between two poles of existence: humans as individual, autonomous moral agents endowed with free will, and humans in need of socializing if they're to achieve their 'highest potential as a culture-creating species' (6). The overarching ethical goal of broadcasting was precisely the continuing attempt to hold these forces in tension. This neo-Victorian passion for improving the lot of those below certainly did nothing to change the balance of power in society. But if public service broadcasting was authoritarian, it also had a conscience.

In the end, of course, it was a set of practical arrangements which ensured an inchoate philosophy was turned into more enduring principles. For instance, it was the BBC's legally sanctioned monopoly, granted originally for administrative convenience, which ensured that sweetness and light could prevail among the many. And it was the establishment of a licence fee paid by all households with a radio receiver that helped ensure a large degree of independence from politics and commercial pressure: it meant, quite simply, that the BBC would be under no obligation to pursue any objective other than that of public service. Whereas in a commercial system, programmes would be made to acquire money, in this public system money was henceforth acquired to make programmes. 'However simple, this little epigram articulates the divergence of basic principles, the different philosophical assumptions, on which broadcasting is built' (Tracey, 1998: 18). The BBC – by the end of the 1920s a corporation, rather than a company, and with a Royal Charter – had a degree of permanence. It was the creation of the state but existed independent of it, hovering in that narrow but fertile space somewhere between 'Nation' and 'People' – a model very quickly adopted, with only minor variation, in many other countries, especially across Western Europe and, further afield, in parts of the British Empire, such as India, Australia, Canada, New Zealand and South Africa. In most cases, these nascent broadcasting organizations shared a set of ethical goals, for public service broadcasting is not about technology: 'It is', as Tracey puts it, 'about an idea, which happens to employ a technology, of how one creates and feeds a society and its culture' (16). That idea is complex and not entirely coherent. Rarely has it existed perfectly formed. Nor has it pretended to offer a quick fix: 'The Enlightenment project was founded upon the limits of human reason and was therefore concerned with emancipation as an always partial project, not an achieved and total fact' (Garnham, 2000: 8). Henceforth, though, wherever broadcasting could guarantee a range, depth, quality and independence of programming for all listeners, it was thought it might become something extraordinary: something which, in a true Enlightenment spirit, would help each one of us find our 'best self' and live a good life.

2 Democracy: Politics, Public Opinion and Debate

If, as I have argued, public service broadcasting's fundamental goal is advancing human enlightenment, then the most important manifestation of this goal is surely its concern with the smooth running of democracy. For in a democracy, everyone's opinion should count. And the Enlightenment ideal demands that our opinions do not just fight against each other, the loudest voice – or even the majority attitude – silencing all others in a vigorous marketplace of ideas. It requires that our opinions be justified, realistic, tolerant of dissent and, not least, freely exchanged. In short, our opinions need to make sense and they need to play fair. Public service broadcasting therefore asserts, even if only implicitly, the value of a deliberative, rational process – where opinions form slowly, through intelligent debate, argument and reflection. Of course, both political history and psychology show opinions that are often an admixture of gut instinct, habit, prejudice or hearsay. But if so, the history of public service broadcasting becomes one of attempted correctives to real-world failures. It is the story of a concerted – if troubled – effort to steer us away from our baser instincts, to shift opinion formation from the instinctive and destructive to the rational and socially useful.

Underpinning all this is the notion of an information deficit in modern life. It is no coincidence that broadcasting was born just as the vote was first being conceded to the majority of adult men and women. Universal suffrage represented a dramatic expansion in the number of people whose views actually counted. Broadcasting 'enabled men and women to take an interest in many issues from which they had previously been excluded', so that, as Reith himself put it, 'a new and mighty weight of public opinion' could emerge (Reith, 1924: 4; Scannell, 2000: 4). This was not just about the free supply of information. Quality mattered as much as quantity. It has long been hoped that 'in a democracy, no one group or set of interests is systematically preferred over another and that the information available to citizens is accurate and impartial' (Street, 2001: 16). Here, too, public service broadcasting has presented itself as tackling a pre-existing deficit. In a much quoted speech delivered in 1931, the British Prime Minister Stanley Baldwin pinpointed how newspapers were too often the personal mouthpieces of wealthy and interfering figures, becoming 'engines of propaganda for the constantly changing policies, desires, personal wishes, personal likes and dislikes' of their owners. Reith's early hope was that broadcasting would allow people to circumvent 'the dictated and partial version of others' so they could make up their own minds (Reith, 1924: 4; Scannell, 2001: 4). This is why a core concern of public service broadcasting from the very beginning has been the notion that it fails to act in the service of the public unless it offers a thoroughly non-partisan approach to reporting the world. This is why 'impartiality' becomes the central issue for us at this stage. It is a tricky concept, because it brings in its wake a whole raft of other interrelated terms: bias, truth, balance, neutrality, objectivity, fairness and so on. None of these is quite the same thing as the others. But they overlap. And all of them come into play when discussing the special claims of public service broadcasting as a democratic force.

Perhaps the most crucial element of public service, however – and one often missed – is its dynamic function: its attempt to nurture an active audience empowered to think for itself. Again, this is an idea with deep roots. Take the following passage from Reith's mission statement, *Broadcast over Britain*:

> We often dislike things intensely, or rather persuade ourselves that we do, when we have actually never been brought into contact with them, and really know nothing whatever about them. On the first occasion when, perforce, we are brought up against them, we are quite sure that our antipathy was justified, but next time perhaps they do not seem so bad, and so gradually we may even come to appreciate them.
>
> (1924: 123)

Through broadcasting, Reith believed, the public's inclination to know more would be 'awakened, stimulated and encouraged' (132). A listener, for instance, might seek out newspaper articles, read books, attend meetings or public talks, and thus slowly but inexorably gain greater insight into the affairs of the day. In this way, the seed 'sown in the twentieth century', Reith promised, 'will bear its fruit in centuries to come' (181). As Briggs points out, this was a conception of the audience not as an inert mass to be 'filled up' with information or 'correct' opinions, but as a living thing 'capable of growth and development' (1995, v.1: 218).

In America, too, the first decades of broadcasting were characterized by what David Goodman (2011) calls a 'civic paradigm'. This meant that while radio was overwhelmingly commercial, it also carried in its DNA a small but significant strand of public-mindedness when it came to topical debate. Once the Federal Communications Commission (FCC) had been told, as it was in 1934, that, for democracy to endure America needed a citizenry 'alive to the problems that are pressing for solution, and able to express, both at election times and between times, an intelligent opinion on these issues', the goal, among progressives at least, was quite clear: ordinary people's engagement with public life, their ability to become 'active, responsive, opinionated and individualized', would have to be 'socially produced'. This, in turn, was something that might be done most efficiently by the new 'mass' medium of radio. Hence, for example, CBS's Lyman Bryson – a key architect of the civic paradigm – argued that Americans needed to get from broadcasting 'experiences that will bring out of them their best qualities, build up their powers, and force them into growth' (76). And many years later, with the imminent launch of America's National Public Radio (NPR) in 1970, we find in *its* mission statement almost exactly the same goal: to use broadcasting to 'promote personal growth ... [and] encourage a sense of active, constructive participation rather than apathetic helplessness' (Ledbetter, 1997: 117). So while British broadcasting deployed *un*democratic means to achieve democratic ends, the founding vision of broadcasting in America was surprisingly familiar: that it, too, might compel people towards freedom.

Public service broadcasting's ambitious commitment to the emancipatory effects of news coverage has been clear from the outset, then. But successful implementation is what matters. The key question is this: How exactly have broadcasters tried to supply 'reliable' information, or maintain a 'non-partisan' approach, or nurture 'intelligent opinion' *in practice*? Any answer entails a long history of trial and error – as well as profound disagreement.

Take impartiality. One means of adopting it has been to supply news that somehow rises above the mucky fray of daily political controversy. In the 1920s and 1930s, this manifested itself in Reith's assertion that in broadcasting 'only those who have a claim to be heard above their fellows on any particular subject' should reach the airwaves (Briggs, 1995, v.1: 232). In other words, news was a matter of listening to authoritative accounts. Half a century or so later another version of this somewhat Olympian model was articulated by one of Reith's successors at the BBC, John Birt. In 1975 Birt had co-authored a series of articles about what he called the systematic 'Bias against Understanding' in television news, with events – as he saw them – forever being reported as isolated incidents without the necessary context. After joining the BBC in 1987, he sought to change this by insisting that the Corporation's news programmes provided more expert-led analysis and introduced more specialist correspondents. Again, the solution was to focus on the significant rather than the ephemeral; to rise above the daily cut and thrust of 'ordinary' journalism (Hendy, 2007: 160, 285). In America, news coverage on NPR has similarly been tilted towards a heavy diet of 'Congressional hearings, press conferences, cabinet secretary interviews' and the like, so that its centre of gravity has been in political and economic affairs, often within the Washington DC Beltway (Ledbetter, 1997: 119–20).

We can see the problem here. If news becomes defined solely as anything of 'significance' that happens within such elite circles, the obvious danger is that, far from being impartial, a certain establishment way of seeing the world gets reinforced. Or even that, as the writer Tom Wolfe once complained, a 'pale beige' kind of journalism prevails: calm and detached, yes, but also bland and uninvolving (1975: 31–5, 47). Wolfe himself suggested that the obvious solution was for journalism to adopt a radically different aesthetic of immediacy and immersion – conveying the feelings and subjective viewpoints of those caught up in events as they happened. In other words, a journalism that could be more captivating – less sterile – through being less detached.

Broadcasters, though, have never simply been forced to choose between a detached position 'above' controversy on the one hand, and subjective, colourful reportage on the other. The challenge has been to convey the vigorous, clamouring voice of democracy while still claiming to remain utterly non-partisan. The most obvious tactic to achieve this has simply been to widen radically the selection of material on air. It was public-minded broadcasters in America who first embraced the idea that airing a multiplicity of views was 'a public good in itself', and that democracy meant making audiences feel more involved (Goodman, 2011: 76–9). Much of the BBC's history since the days of Reith has been a story of learning – sometimes from America, sometimes from its own audiences, sometimes from its own instincts – how to achieve both this democratic 'communicative style' and the airing of a multiplicity of views.

Whichever approach is adopted, major pitfalls await the public broadcaster. Being detached avoids overt partisanship; but it can also end up with a narrow range of voices conveying establishment values.

Allowing a radically wider range of opinions to appear on air creates an authentic feel of democratic debate; but it also demands broadcasters ensure the most strident voices don't always prevail, or that minor differences of opinion don't become exaggerated or that ill-founded arguments aren't given equal weight to well-founded ones. Presenting news in a familiar and engaging manner might draw listeners and viewers towards a greater involvement with public affairs; but – to quote a familiar expression – simply satisfying what the public is interested *in* is not the same as supplying what is in the 'public interest'. In navigating this tricky terrain public service broadcasters are in a radically different position to their commercial rivals. They do not just have to provide better-quality radio or television news. Their public status means they also have a duty towards the health of the wider civic realm. Indeed, if they have worked hard to establish a reputation for truthfulness, *what* they say (and *how* they say it) will almost certainly have a correspondingly greater impact on the running of democracy itself – for good or ill.

Two brief examples illustrate how troublesome this role can be. First: the so-called 'Gilligan' affair, which led to official disquiet over journalistic standards at the BBC in 2003 and 2004. In this case, one of the reporters employed by the Corporation's flagship *Today* programme, Andrew Gilligan, had claimed on air that the United Kingdom government had ordered a key security dossier to be 'sexed up' in order to exaggerate the threat posed by the Iraqi leader Saddam Hussein – a claim that suggested the government was falsifying the case for war. For many observers, Gilligan had revealed a vital truth about government 'spin' being out of control. But amid the turbulence that followed the reporter's claim, it also emerged that he did not have a full contemporaneous record of a crucial conversation with a government advisor and that the *Today* programme's own editor had privately expressed concern over his 'loose use of language'. The government-appointed Hutton Inquiry into the whole affair therefore concluded that Gilligan's central claim was 'unfounded' (Hendy, 2007: 398). Clearly, the discomfort of the government was neither here nor there: it would have been perfectly appropriate – that is, in the *public interest* – to embarrass any government caught lying. 'Neutrality' is irrelevant when choosing between truth and falsehood. However, several observers, notably the *Financial Times'* John Lloyd, thought the episode revealed a much more serious failing. Not only was it all 'carelessly done' when the BBC should have been setting a gold standard for accuracy; the Corporation had increasingly fallen for the cynical assumption that all politicians were born liars and rogues. The kind of confrontational jousting practised by the *Today* programme in particular – which no doubt made it 'involving' – also betrayed a journalism 'ravenous for conflict'. As a result, the BBC, instead of providing reportage that was detailed, subtle, rational, courteous, was contributing to a growing 'anomie and distrust within civil society' (Lloyd, 2004: 2–24, 89, 187–95).

Our second example illustrates vividly the kind of discourse that sometimes exists when 'subtle, rational, courteous' reportage is pushed to the margins of the civic realm. In January 2011, the US Democrat Congresswomen Gabrielle Giffords was shot in the head by a disturbed gunman while meeting voters in Arizona. The local sheriff quickly pointed out that not only had the leading Republican Sarah Palin been circulating a campaign poster showing Giffords in the crosshairs of a rifle, but that a constant and vitriolic rhetoric of hate had been relentlessly directed at Democrats such as Giffords by Republican and Tea Party supporters through media outlets such as Fox News and talk radio. In fact, there was no evidence that the man who shot Giffords was directly influenced by anything he heard or saw on television or radio. Yet it was reasonable to see the whole affair as symbolic of an increasingly partisan and hysterical media atmosphere having poisoned political debate. Indeed, this was confirmed by the vicious arguments about who was to 'blame' conducted by both sides over the nation's airwaves in the days that followed. As with the Gilligan affair in Britain, there appeared to be a deeper issue: what the historian Stephen Miller has seen as a serious decline in the 'art' of civilized conversation. This, he reminds us, depends for its good working on listening as much as on talking. But when tuning in to commercial talk radio, all he ever heard was a slew of 'anger communities' at war: bombasts and zealots out to confirm existing opinions rather than challenge them (Miller, 2006: 267–304).

Here, then, we can see the case for the civic paradigm's calm and deliberative approach put rather eloquently – in this instance through its very absence. As with the Gilligan affair in Britain, we are reminded that when we discuss the practices of news coverage, we have to go beyond our traditional focus on bias and neutrality and start to explore the much wider and deeper civic role inherent to the 'public–ness' of public service broadcasting.

Detachment or Demoticism?

The civic role that Reith had in mind when he established news coverage on the BBC in the 1920s emerged in a curious manner, for, as Seaton points out, the organization he led was actually founded on a rejection of politics. It saw politics as intrinsically divisive, and broadcasting as intrinsically unifying. Reith wanted to give listeners 'access to the discourses of public life' – which was why he pressed hard for the BBC to be allowed to broadcast live coverage of debates in Parliament as well as the great occasions of state (Scannell and Cardiff, 1991: 13; 27). At the same time, he disliked party politics, sensing that beneath the thin veneer of civilized argument there lurked a deep well of antagonism. For him governance was a matter of efficient administration: public affairs should and could be managed by an elite of clever and disinterested public servants – people such as, well, himself (Curran and Seaton, 1997: 115). This same elevated conception of broadcasting as unifying national force is woven through all subsequent BBC thinking. In the 1970s, for instance, we find its Director-General, Charles Curran, reminding staff that in covering industrial disputes the BBC should, if anything, be biased in favour of 'the resolution, in circumstances of tolerance, of the differences of view' which had arisen. Since it was 'the child of parliamentary democracy', he concluded, its job was to quench fires rather than stoke them (Hendy, 2007: 90–3). Nevertheless, industrial disputes could never be ignored altogether. Back in 1926, indeed, it had been the General Strike that had first revealed in stunning fashion the public appetite for up-to-date news and propelled the BBC into hurriedly creating – and thereafter steadily expanding – its own news-gathering department. The Company's coverage of the Strike, though hardly 'neutral', had certainly risen above the hysterically one-sided reporting from Winston Churchill's crude pro-government *British Gazette*. A notably less partisan model of reporting had therefore been tried and tested. Representing 'both' sides of a debate was not only an effective way of dealing with the dangerous territory of 'controversy'; it also became a defining feature of public service broadcasting's whole approach to political coverage during normal service. In the end, the BBC emerged from the Strike with an ethic of political neutrality.

An ambivalent relationship with government had also been stripped bare, however. The BBC might claim to have been representing the 'nation' rather more than the 'government'. But then – and since – it has been required to keep at least one eye on the political mood of the day. The very real prospect of an imminent Whitehall take-over in 1926 had only been seen off through the BBC censoring itself. And Reith's own famously cautious attitude has always made it easy to see here a history of debilitating deference and the wilful avoidance of contro-versy. In 1970, for instance, the academic Stuart Hall wrote that the

BBC's problem was not one of devious reporters deliberately slanting news, but an inbuilt, almost unconscious bias towards the status quo in the way news programmes were being produced. More recently, the documentary filmmaker Adam Curtis has argued that 'Most journalism at the BBC is still stuck with the idea that power goes through Westminster' (*Sunday Times*, 22 May 2011). Yet, in many respects, the BBC has been more sinned against than sinning when it comes to its relationship with politicians. In Reith's day, it was the politicians who imposed on the BBC a restricted range of what could be reported. It was also the politicians, not the broadcasters, who rigidly defined the notion of balance: for them, balancing viewpoints never really extended beyond a requirement to feature the three main constitutional parties. Opinion well to the left or to the right of these parties, even if quite widely held, was simply not acceptable. No wonder the BBC struggled to get more radical or unpredictable views on air.

Fortunately, however, this diminished conception of broadcasting's democratic role did not go unchallenged for long. In his biography of the BBC's Head of Talks programmes under Reith, Hilda Matheson, Michael Carney quotes a draft letter Matheson wrote to Reith in which she suggested that there were two policies available to a monopolistic broadcasting service:

> either to take the middle, traditional, orthodox view on most things with a minimum of latitude on either side of that line, or to express all the most important currents of thought on both sides, preserving a carefully balanced diversity.

As far as Matheson was concerned, 'the second option was the only one which could bring the public in touch with important formative influences'. And if every subject was tackled 'with sympathy and imagination, the right speakers and the right tone' then no subject could be beyond discussion (Carney, 1999: 75–6). This spirited advocacy is an important corrective to our traditional view of the early BBC. It shows us that the multiplicity of views and the 'free play' of ideas which Goodman sees as characterizing American radio's civic paradigm was also being advanced within the supposedly more restrictive BBC. It also reminds us that, while Reith was clearly the dominant figure in early BBC history, he wasn't the only figure shaping its editorial thinking. Pressure for change often came from within the institution, as well as without.

We probably need, though, to acknowledge the continuing presence of two somewhat contradictory forces within BBC thinking over the past ninety years. One, the desire to be aloof from divisive petty politics, has seen the BBC drawn towards a somewhat top-heavy 'national', conciliatory role – which, whatever its merits, has also entailed papering over some very real cracks in the social fabric and, on occasion, an uncomfortably close relationship to politicians. The other, a desire for an almost Miltonic freedom of expression, has seen the BBC willing to embrace a diversity of viewpoints and even offend the political class. These are not necessarily mutually contradictory behaviours. In a sense, they are two aspects of the public service mission: to somehow represent the nation to itself in a coherent way, and to somehow represent that nation in all its diversity and plurality. There is no doubt, though, that over time the most important shift in editorial values – not just at the BBC but across all forms of public service broadcasting – has been the steady widening of the range of people, voices, opinions, subject matter and styles allowed on air. In other words, the broadcasters' understanding of democracy has become more demotic. It has taken more account of ordinary people's opinions, and it has included a more accessible set of communicative styles.

It has been suggested that two factors more than any others propelled the BBC into this closer relationship with the public: the belated appearance of commercial competition, and the arrival of the new medium of television. For example, in what James Curran calls the 'populist narrative', the arrival of ITV in 1955 is seen as a seminal moment in Britain. With its lively, less deferential style and its portrayals of working-class life in series such as *Coronation Street* (1960–), commercial television threatened to steal a national audience that a complacent BBC had assumed was its own. So, the narrative goes, competition – combined with the innately entertaining style of television – spurred the BBC into become less deferential. This version of history also points to the influence of American broadcasting values. The vox-pops, raucous, unscripted town hall debates and phone-ins that had appeared regularly on American radio and television stations since the 1930s are seen as having provided a model of vigorously demotic debate which the BBC simply could not keep ignoring (Loviglio, 2005).

But there is another, 'liberal', narrative, which suggests that the long-term shift to a more demotic register has arisen organically within public service broadcasting. For instance, a verité approach could be discerned in the social documentaries of pioneering BBC producers such as Olive Shapley, who, as early as the 1930s – a full two decades before the launch of ITV – took outside broadcast vans around the north of England to record the experiences and views of ordinary men and women in their own homes or workplaces. Later, in the final stages of the Second World War, BBC reporters equipped with portable recorders sent back vivid on-location accounts of the D-Day landings for *War Report* (Starkey and Crisell, 2009: 6). Indeed, the war represented a crucial phase in the BBC's development, since the need to secure home-front morale and a steady audience for its news output encouraged programme-makers to find new, more welcoming ways of speaking to their audience.

The 1960s almost certainly represented a second crucial stage. By the end of the decade, we find that, just as in America NPR's news magazine *All Things Considered* (1971) was busy covering anti-Vietnam War protests through a colourful collage of voices, chanting on the streets and surveillance helicopters circling overhead (Ledbetter, 1997: 117–18), in Britain, the BBC's lunchtime news and current affairs programme *The World at One* (1965–) was regularly conveying the same *feel* of what was happening during various tumultuous events across Europe, through 'packages' enriched with rough-hewn actuality and the voices of ordinary people (Hendy, 2007: 49). The tape-recorder – small, portable, unobtrusive – allowed ordinary people, unused to public exposure, to speak easily and naturally in their own environments – it was 'a technical means to the democratization of the radio subject' (Scannell, 1979: 104). The BBC's new demotic style could be pinpointed to an even earlier date through its coverage of national politics on television. Take, for example, Grace Wyndham Goldie and the team of iconoclastic journalists she led in producing ground-breaking series such as *Tonight* (1957–65) – a current affairs magazine which by 1960 regularly attracted 9 million viewers for its original blend of politics and light entertainment and its incisive style of interviewing. It was, as Crisell says, very clearly 'on the side of the viewer' (2002: 99). Indeed, Grace Wyndham Goldie herself explained *Tonight*'s philosophy thus: it was designed to show that 'It was not always necessary to be respectful; experts were not invariably right; the opinions of those in high places did not have to be accepted' (100). Coming from the BBC, with its image of Reithian obsequiousness, this was a stunning shift in tone. When the 1962–3 programme, *That Was the Week That Was* offered BBC television viewers a fiercely satirical take on the week's events and ridiculed politicians relentlessly, it did *not* come out of the blue: it emerged from a longer, deeper tradition of irreverence and critique.

This tradition was responsible, over time, for enhancing not just the idea of public accountability, but also a kind of public sensibility – one capable of compassion. What Scannell calls television's 'social eye' is an essential component of this. At first, he points out, British television offered a 'panorama of actualities', including sport and the ritual events of royalty and the state; political reporting, too, began as 'a service essentially for politicians – a means whereby they aired or debated their views before the viewing public or (in a strictly non-partisan way of course) educated the television audience on contemporary world affairs' (1979: 98). Potentially contentious social issues – housing, unemployment, prostitution, delinquency, old age, etc. – *were* covered, though not through news or current affairs but rather through new kinds of documentaries. In looking back at these, Scannell suggests, we find 'the social subject is structured from *our* point of view (i.e. the audience), and our concerns with current problem areas in our society' (97). When, for instance, the BBC investigated the problems and concerns of contemporary youth for a 1952 programme, five months of research was devoted not to gathering interviews with politicians or experts but to travelling all over Britain, 'meeting teenagers at work in shops, factories and offices; talking to them in their homes, in canteens, hostels, dance halls, cinema queues and youth clubs' (102). This, of course, was all part of an established documentary ethos of building a story 'bottom-up' through actuality – an ethos developed before the Second World War in radio, photography and film. So neither television nor the BBC 'invented' documentary as such. Nevertheless, documentaries such as this show how the BBC, through its television service, exhibited the kind of genuinely populist impulse pursued elsewhere by, say, the British *Picture Post* magazine or the CBS series *See It Now* (1951–8) in America. Indeed, in picking the former North Region and war reporter Robert Reid as the presenter of its new investigative documentary series *Special Enquiry* (1991–2), the BBC's editor Norman Swallow declared quite explicitly that Reid was 'no routine spokesman of the Establishment, but a man to be trusted – one of "us" rather than one of "them"' (104). Broadcasting, in other words, was no longer a form of speaking *at* the public; it was a means of speaking as if it represented the public itself. All this, let us remember, was before the supposedly game-changing arrival of commercial television in 1955.

We can say, then, that over time public service broadcasting has come, in Scannell's words, 'to fulfil – never without difficulty, always under pressure – its role as an independent "public sphere" and a forum for open public discussion of matters of general concern' (2000: 58). It has done this by carefully balancing the two editorial imperatives that have been there from the start: on the one hand, to somehow bind the nation and to nurture a collective climate of rational opinion formation

– a position that involves a degree of 'top-down' selection and editorial initiative – and on the other, to represent not just some but *all* the people who constitute the nation, whatever the imperfections of their thought or behaviour – a position that involves holding up a mirror to society.

This precarious combination, in which public broadcasters somehow both reflect *and* lead, can still be seen at work in the editorial codes of conduct by which journalists are supposed to operate today. The BBC's guidelines, for instance, describe how the organization must serve the public interest by reporting 'stories of significance' through 'specialist expertise' bringing 'authority and analysis to the complex world in which we live'; stories have to be 'well sourced' and based on 'sound evidence' (BBC, 2010: 4). Elsewhere, BBC documents explain that 'senior journalists' are entitled to reach clear conclusions, provided they have the evidence to support a particular interpretation: there's no requirement to be even-handed between truth and falsehood (BBC, 2011: 7–8). All this articulates very clearly a continuing respect for professional selectivity. But there are also other, more demotic strictures. Thus, impartiality – which is stated explicitly as being 'at the core' of the BBC's values – must be applied to *all* subject matters, and must 'reflect a breadth and diversity of opinion' such that 'no significant strand of thought is knowingly unreflected or underrepresented'. 'We aim to reflect the world as it is', the guidelines say. And the world will always be reflected in a 'clear' and accessible manner (3–5). This speaks eloquently of a more egalitarian, inclusive definition of public affairs.

Over the last two decades it is this second, more egalitarian approach that has had greater momentum. As a result, impartiality itself is changing as a concept. In the early days it applied almost exclusively to party politics and industrial disputes. As one recent BBC policy document put it, this 'involved keeping a balance to ensure the seesaw did not tip too far to one side or another'. But, the document goes on to say, 'In today's multi-polar Britain, with its range of cultures, beliefs and identities, impartiality involves many more than two sides to an argument.' Instead of a seesaw, there is impartiality as a 'wagon wheel' – not quite circular, and with spokes that 'go in all directions' (BBC, 2007: 5). What this rather tortured metaphor means in practice is that impartiality is not just about even-handedness and objectivity, or even about occupying a safe centre ground: it is about 'breadth of view and completeness' – something 'achieved by bringing extra perspectives to bear, rather than limiting horizons or censoring opinion' (6–7). In other words, public service broadcasting has attempted to renegotiate the definitions of 'inclusivity' in a way that moves it beyond bipolar models of Left and Right, True or False, Black or White. Formally, at least, it has sought instead to encompass some of real life's shifting shades of grey.

The Challenges of Inclusivity

A more demotic kind of public broadcasting only brings new stresses and strains into the system. It's worth asking, for example, if broadcasting's more intimate and less deferential style – whatever its merits – distorts our understanding of what is truly significant in political life. And in shifting away from the interpretation of events by authoritative figures and becoming more interested in what 'ordinary' people think, might it be argued that public service broadcasting has slipped from a badly needed pluralism into a less welcome relativism, where no single person's opinions are any more valid than anyone else's and where values or truth become utterly elusive?

Take, first, the question of politics having become personalized. Placing politicians under closer scrutiny in election campaigns seems, on the face of it, to be an entirely positive development. But there have been downsides, too. One classic study of political reporting on television, for example, focused on the British General Election of 1964 – and, specifically on how public attitudes to the three main party leaders changed in the course of the campaign (Blumler and McQuail, 1968). The analysis showed that, overall, the Conservative leader Sir Alec Douglas-Home lost ground while his opponents, the Labour leader Harold Wilson and the Liberal leader Jo Grimond, both gained ground. There appeared to be a number of factors in this shift – especially, it seemed, voters' perceptions of the three politicians' relative qualities of strength and forcefulness. The fact that Douglas-Home lost ground might, of course, simply reflect a pre-existing reality, namely that the Conservative leader was intrinsically less impressive and extended scrutiny by the media served the public interest by revealing this. The pertinent point here, however, is that the leaders were all being assessed by voters for their *character*, rather than their politics. There was a striking parallel in Britain's 2010 General Election, which featured the country's first live televized debates between the main party leaders. Each of the 2010 debates focused heavily on matters of policy. But most coverage – and most public reaction – focused on the *performance* of the candidates, the way they addressed the audience, their body language and so on. Despite his reputation for being in command of economic policy, the Labour leader, Gordon Brown, came across badly: convoluted in his speech, failing to 'connect'. The Conservative leader, David Cameron, performed as expected for a former public relations manager: he was emollient. The most dramatic audience response, however, was to the Liberal Democrat leader, Nick Clegg, who surged overnight in the approval ratings, having spent the first debate talking to questioners in the studio on first-name terms and addressing viewers at home by looking directly at the camera. This personable style encouraged voters to rate him highly for honesty and conviction, and was deemed so successful that it led to a blatant shift in tactics by the two other party leaders in later debates. As it happened, Clegg's own dramatic lead in the polls wasn't sustained for the duration of the campaign. But neither was it entirely ephemeral in its effects. It was enough to help him secure the post of Deputy Prime Minister in the subsequent Conservative-led coalition government – and to then rapidly abandon various pre-election pledges soon after. Unsurprisingly, having so blatantly destroyed his recently won reputation for honesty and conviction, his opinion-ratings fell dramatically, only months after his extraordinary television triumph. It was as though his television performance had been a dream, a moment of mass delusion.

At one level, the live TV election debates of 2010 can be seen as a particular example of a more general problem with television that has been identified by Andrew Crisell (2004): that images *mislead*. This is partly because they are themselves 'inchoate and ambiguous in meaning', partly because they are superficial – that is, they attend, as it were, to the surface of things – and partly because they are often provided for emotional rather than informational impact (7–8). The challenge here for public service broadcasting, then, is to ensure that the perfectly legitimate desire to engage an audience is always accompanied by an equally forceful desire to add informational or, better still, analytical value. The lines between engagement and understanding are, however, frequently blurred for, although television's 'social eye' has an egalitarian feel about it, the blurring of the public and the private has come at a price. Those public figures busy being 'authentic' are fully aware they're being watched – there's always an element of self-consciousness involved, a performance even. Because of this, we now have to distinguish between those who are sincere and those who are 'doing' sincere: the ravenous hunger to get behind the rehearsed performance intensifies. So a downward spiral, where interviewer and interviewee enact a kind of theatrical duel with each other, testing for weakness and slip-ups, can often be heard, for example, on Radio 4's *Today* – so much so that one senior politician claimed in 1996 that he could no longer 'communicate either what is a legitimate political point or what is actually the news story that got him the invitation on to the programme in the first place' (Hendy, 2007: 323–5).

More seriously, perhaps, this blurring of public and private and the parallel shift towards a probing of character arguably threatens our very understanding of politics – thus undermining a core ambition of public service broadcasting. The problem, essentially, is one of distraction. Character and personality are, as we have seen, things that can be captured on screen – indeed politicians, knowing they are under constant scrutiny, make themselves accessible on the understanding that to appear detached or impersonal comes across as suspiciously buttoned up and undemocratic. What can't so easily be captured on screen, though, is the steady grind of politicians' real work: changing things through committees and councils, the lengthy drafting of policies, the cumulative effect of thousands of minor acts and compromises. This grind is the essence of public life. But according to the sociologist Richard Sennett (1977), our understanding of it has been slowly destroyed by what he calls the 'tyranny of intimacy'. He traces the origins of this to the nineteenth century and earlier – so broadcasting isn't his main concern. But what he describes implicates broadcasting, particularly television, because this focus on personality is something that's clearly been amplified by the modern mass media. The problem, Sennett suggests, is that we have come to judge the performance of figures in public office – something that should be assessed with dispassionate detachment – according to irrelevant criteria concerning their private lives. Similarly, the political theorist David Runciman (2008), in exploring what most of us refer to as 'political hypocrisy' – that is, a mismatch between what a politician says and what she or he does – suggests we have become dangerously intolerant of failure. In reality, he reminds us, good people sometimes perform bad acts and bad people sometimes perform good acts. Yet political broadcasting no longer allows for this possibility. The key point is this: that to explain politics through questions of character is dangerously distracting and reductionist. It takes our focus away from the actual actions of politicians – and it encourages politicians to do the same. Sennett suggests we need to restore a sense of dispassionate detachment. In the meantime, it is as if we – and those who work in broadcasting – have forgotten some of the warnings issued back in the 1930s and 1940s. It was then that a generation of researchers in the United States – Theodor Adorno, Paul Lazarsfeld, Hadley Cantril, Gordon Allport and others – examined the reaction of listeners to 'charismatic' broadcasters such as Father Coughlin, and found that they responded, often uncritically, to the 'human touch' of a warm and engaging voice, even if it was selling them snake oil (Cantril and Allport, 1935). The conclusion back then was that it should henceforth be the role of responsible broadcasters not to collude with this power but to resist it. Which is why the issue of intimacy presents a direct challenge to public service broadcasting even today. Its demotic appeal is obvious, and it's clearly a duty of an institution such as the BBC to engage us. But this effort needs balancing with that other recurrent mission: to help us grow into more rational beings, capable of treating what we hear and see with proper scepticism.

Here, then, we come to the second major issue to arise from public service broadcasters' embrace of inclusivity: the danger of legitimate pluralism sliding into a more problematic relativism – and thus the prospect of objective truths or universal values disappearing entirely. This speaks to a wider social phenomenon. The cultural observer Susan Jacoby, for instance, describes in her book *The Age of American Unreason* (2008), a long-term trend of increasing popular contempt for expert opinion, fuelled, she suggests, by a credo that 'places all opinions on an equal footing' (211). The mass media are especially complicit in this, she suggests, since they are 'first and foremost among the vectors of anti-intellectualism' (10). Why? Because in regarding anything 'controversial' as worth covering, in regarding personal conviction as being as valuable as critical judgement, and in believing that all sides of an issue must be given equal space on air, they normalize ideas that 'ought to be dismissed as the province of a lunatic fringe' (20). So, for example, in giving climate-change sceptics equality with qualified climate scientists – the vast majority of whom regard the impact of human activity on the climate as proven – or, again, in giving religious advocates of 'intelligent design' equality with trained biologists who are able to demonstrate the reality of evolution, a genuine distortion of truth takes place. As Jacoby says, you can't 'place observable scientific facts, subject to proof, on the same level as un-provable supernatural fantasy' (21). But of course you can – and many television and radio programmes frequently do, in adherence to a mistaken sense of 'balance'.

Even the BBC hasn't been immune to this relativist trap. In July 2011, for instance, it was forced to acknowledge that 'due impartiality' hadn't always been observed in its science reporting. The geneticist Professor Steven Jones described the Corporation's overall commitment to science as 'exemplary'. But one incident stood out. When a journal article published in 1998 had suggested there might be a link between the 'MMR' (Measles-Mumps-Rubella) vaccine given routinely to children and the onset of autism, BBC journalists had felt obliged to reflect the press reaction and the widespread health scare which followed. As it happened, the original research was flawed. But in any case the overwhelming medical consensus was that no link could be found between the MMR vaccine and autism – and that the health benefits of the vaccine far outweighed the risks. Despite this, journalists at the BBC had apparently interpreted their requirement to reflect all sides with due impartiality as meaning that they had to give about as much airtime to those who worried about MMR as they were giving to those who defended it. This, Professor Jones concluded, amounted to giving 'undue attention to marginal opinion' (BBC, 2011a: 5). And this mattered, because of its subsequent impact on public opinion. A survey conducted at the time showed that 'most people felt that because both sides of the argument had been given equal time by the media, then there must be equal evidence for both': 'An attempt to be impartial had exactly the opposite result' – and, in the end, the rate of vaccine take-up fell sharply, destroying hard-won herd immunity (61). The underlying problem, it seems, wasn't just the understandable desire of the BBC to give 'equality of voice' to all sections of society. It was also that journalists had been reluctant to listen to expert opinions – both within the BBC and in the scientific community at large (5).

This represents a serious criticism. But it needs to be put into perspective. Jones acknowledges that, even in the case of MMR, 'the BBC was far from the worst culprit' (60). He also notes that in subsequent coverage of an influenza epidemic, the BBC had successfully avoided hyperbole – 'in contrast to that of certain overseas broadcasters who sowed something close to terror' (61). One reason for this, perhaps, is that the Corporation had since decided to strengthen its contacts with the scientific community, improve the training of its journalists, and appoint an overall Science Editor who would assess the weight of news coverage 'relative to the weight of scientific work' (6). Most importantly of all, it had ruled that programme-makers would henceforth be required to distinguish 'between well-established fact and opinion' (8). This declaration – and the process of scrutiny from which it emerged – suggests that the accountability expected of public service broadcasting often leads to the creation of a workable 'self-correcting' mechanism.

Indeed, when it comes to its historic role in nurturing democracy, we might conclude that the BBC is actually in a perpetual state of self-correction. As Scannell points out, in broadcasting, the extent of openness or inclusivity – and how it is interpreted – is 'something that varies according to the social, economic, and political climate': 'The thresholds of tolerance are not fixed' (2000: 58). It's likely, for instance, that British television was more 'open' in the permissive climate of the mid-1960s than it was in the late 1970s. Quite possibly, it's going through another shift, from relative openness and confidence in the 2000s to a distinctly jittery attitude to questions of bias or language in the 2010s. As always, public service broadcasting needs to sense the overall public mood – and to be no more than one step ahead of it.

This, however, raises a final danger: that in trying constantly to match public mood, broadcasters begin to lose sight of their own vision – that they merely reflect what's going on in the world and react to it. The fashion for 'rolling news' or extended live coverage – with its deliberately minimalist level of editorial interpretation – though now a standard feature of broadcast news, was born of this lack of confidence. Yet impartiality – a commitment to treating all sides fairly – is emphatically not the same as avoiding an editorial judgement or position. As the BBC's Director-General Hugh Carleton Greene pointed out in 1965, the Corporation is not supposed to be 'neutral' when it comes to 'clashes for and against basic moral values – truthfulness, justice, freedom, compassion, tolerance'. 'Being too good "democrats" in these matters', he added, 'could open the way to the destruction of democracy itself' (BBC, 1965: 12).

In the end, therefore, the real challenge for public service broadcasting is not in reflecting democracy, but its role in nourishing it. Where once this was seen as achievable through a simple act of dispensing authoritative information and opinions, we now acknowledge a multiplicity of strategies. The American sociologist Paul Starr, for instance, sees a world of 'intensive and combative' polarities (2010: 95). The solution, he says, is not simply to wring our hands at the loss of old 'norms of detachment' or lament the absence of calm and trusted commentators in the Walter Cronkite mould: 'Democracy needs passion, and partisanship provides it.' He favours a 'fighting public sphere' (98). Starr, however, is assuming here that the only alternative is some form of retrograde 'consensus-building' media, superficially appealing but also a rather bland prospect. Yet there is another alternative. And it's the one that's been attempted, however imperfectly, by the BBC over the course of the second half of the twentieth century: an approach that aims to encompass diversity-within-unity. It aims to make a range of political voices and interpretations available to every citizen. It actively challenges the idea of separate public spheres, and the loss of genuine dialogue that entails, by asserting the value of a shared space where accidental exposure to other points of view can still occur. One classic statement of the strategy came from the Controller of Radio 4, Tony Whitby, writing in 1974:

> We should not allow ourselves to be put in the position of having to demonstrate that broadcasting a certain programme does no damage of any kind; with the implication that if it creates one pennyworth of harm it should therefore not be transmitted. This is an utterly false proposition. *Not* broadcasting certain types of programme is also damaging and the good that we do by airing certain subjects in a responsible way, though it may well be immeasurable, must be set in the balance against any incidental harm … . A broadcasting service which avoids difficult subjects because they create difficult questions of public relations or because they can be shown to have damaging effects in some ways, may be shirking its public responsibilities. Certain questions need to be aired and discussed in a responsible society if that society is to grow in a healthy way.
>
> (BBC WAC, 1974)

The choice of words in that last sentence – 'responsible', 'society', 'grow', 'healthy' – is absolutely key to our understanding of public service broadcasting's complex and troubled relationship with democracy. For, in effect, it rejects the idea that broadcasting is merely at the beck and call of historical forces. Instead, it sees society as something which broadcasting can still act upon – and thus shape for the better. Of course, it can't only see society as something to be acted upon. The element of 'public service' resides in the peculiar mix of standpoints broadcasting can supply at one and the same time: following and leading, reflecting and shaping, expert and demotic, detached and engaged. Above all, though, the 'public service' of public service broadcasting resides in its ability to facilitate 'the participation of different groups in the collective dialogue of society' (Curran and Seaton, 1997: 362). The important contrast is not between an unrestricted form of vigorous expression on one side and a state-controlled or publicly 'directed' one on the other. It's the contrast between a system that seeks to cajole us and one that seeks to supply us with the essential toolkit of democracy: a hefty dose of rational scepticism, an openness of mind and an empathy of spirit.

3 Cultivation: Broadcasting Culture

For those in the commercial sector the cultural task of broadcasting is clear. It is, as far as possible, to provide listeners and viewers with the entertainment that they seem to want – no more, no less. For public service broadcasting the task is more complex – simply because it proceeds from the basis that people's tastes are changeable. Once this is assumed, it's never quite enough to *only* give people what they want. There will also be a 'public good' in giving them what they might want in the future if only they could know about it – perhaps even in giving them what wiser folk think they need. After all, they might come to like it – maybe even demand more and more of it. To put it simply, while commercial broadcasting assumes that in cultural matters demand will be what shapes supply, public service broadcasting assumes that supply might actually be capable of shaping demand.

At the core of this belief has been an assumption that 'culture', like reliable information, is both a precious commodity and something that's been restricted to the lucky few for too long. It needs to be spread around, so that all can share in its benefits. What exactly those benefits are – well, for a long time these have been self-evident. Go back, once again, to Matthew Arnold. He believed that in a secular age, it was surely culture that would make us the fully rounded persons that we should be: exposure to the great works of art, poetry, music and literature could help us rise above our narrow, selfish lives. The key thing was that culture was transcendent, evidence of the timeless unity of the human spirit. It was an oasis of agreed value in a quarrelsome, degenerate world. Which is why culture was seen to be above politics: one had to be a fully formed person first, and a citizen later. Politics was conflict; culture was harmony. So it was culture – then and always – which provided the key to building a new, more graceful world.

Broadcasting rapidly allied itself to this project because, as we saw in Chapter 1, it was born at a moment of intense intellectual anxiety over the deleterious effects of mass culture. As far as Reith was concerned, 'To have exploited so great a scientific invention for the purpose and pursuit of "entertainment" alone would have been a prostitution of its powers and an insult to the character and intelligence of the people' (1924: 17). As LeMahieu says, the BBC's paternalism 'was animated by a genuine idealism' (1988: 147).

Yet if culture as a kind of ethical pedagogy has long been the underlying project of public service broadcasting, it's also long been one fraught with difficulty. As Terry Eagleton points out, 'Culture and crisis go together like Laurel and Hardy' (2000: 37). One simple reason for this is that in asking it to stand in for God or happiness or political justice we almost certainly ask too much of it. Another is that 'Culture' means different things – sometimes contradictory things – to different people. For Reith, taking his cue not just from Arnold but from pretty much the entire generation into which he was born, Culture was unequivocally the 'best in every department of human knowledge, endeavour and achievement' (1924: 34). With Reith we have Culture as aesthetics – pure, unsullied, civilized: 'Culture' with a capital 'C'. But this isn't a definition that can go uncontested for long. As Eagleton argues, Culture thus defined is 'among other things, a way in which a governing order fashions an identity for itself in stone, script and sound, and its effect is to intimidate as well as inspire' (2000: 54). Culture only *appears* to be neutral. 'We are asked to believe that unity is inherently preferable to conflict, or symmetry to one-sidedness', as though 'all passionate conviction was *ipso facto* irrational' (17–18). This suggests that 'refined feelings, well-tempered passions, agreeable manners and an open mind' might end up creating nothing but a mildly conservative liberalism. It is, in other words, a version 'on the side of the mannered middle classes rather than the irate masses' (18). Indeed, Eagleton concludes, we might say that 'in the very act of realizing some human potentials', Culture 'damagingly suppresses others' (23). In the end, its disinterestedness is fraudulent.

There is a much looser definition of culture to hand, of course – a more anthropological definition which sees it not as a narrow cluster of fine artistic works to be appreciated respectfully but as a 'whole way of life'. The writer most closely associated with this wider definition is Raymond Williams, largely through his influential work *Culture and Society* (1958, 2nd edn, 1987). But the anthropological version has deeper roots. It started to take grip in the nineteenth century, when European and American colonialism was busy erasing various 'native' lifestyles across the globe. In these circumstances, culture embodied something of an *antithesis* to Western 'civilization' – what Geoffrey Hartman called an organic 'sociable, populist, and traditional way of life, characterized by a quality that pervades everything and makes a person feel rooted or at home' (1999: 211). During the twentieth century, this definition was brought in-house, so that it could be claimed by Western people, too – especially those who embodied a 'minority' identity, sexual, racial, generational or regional in nature, but also one that was just straightforwardly 'ordinary'. So we could start talking of, say, 'English culture' – consisting, for George Orwell, of 'solid breakfasts and gloomy Sundays, smoky towns, and winding roads and red pillar-boxes', as well as a deeply ingrained hypocrisy, a suspicion of artiness and an obstinate nostalgia (2008: 109–14). As Eagleton suggests, this anthropological culture remained the kind that 'lived on the pulses at a far deeper level than the mind': it was custom, kinship, language, ritual, mythology – all the things which choose *us* rather more than we choose them (2000: 13, 28). And nowadays it can operate at almost any scale. As well as 'English culture' or 'American culture', there's 'African-American culture', 'Northern culture', 'youth culture', 'canteen culture' and so on *ad infinitum*. The main feature, however, is this: that if culture is defined anthropologically, it becomes something we *all* have. And if it's something we all have, the obvious question is this: what can public service broadcasting give us that we don't already have?

One way to answer this question is to turn to broadcasting's own history. Ever since the 1920s, the narrative goes, there's been a steady process of democratization in cultural programming just as in news coverage. Broadcasters have progressively widened their definition of culture, moving steadily from offering just the selected highlights of Western civilization towards a more inclusive version, in which radio and television have increasingly devoted themselves to portraying and discussing popular culture – genre fiction, soaps, pop music or garden makeovers, say – and so pushing the 'high' arts of opera, dance, classical music, literary fiction and the rest to the margins, where a minority can find them if they need to. A value shift is part of this narrative, too, since culture has always been part normative as well as part descriptive. So whereas in Reith's day, broadcasting could be said to have been offering the 'best' through giving listeners access to the most refined and celebrated achievements of humanity, in the later twentieth century it could be said to have been offering the 'best' by giving viewers and listeners access to the most *authentic* examples of culture and lifestyles. More than that, we could even say that a broadcaster such as the BBC has shifted from a reluctant acceptance of the need to portray popular culture to a full-blooded embrace of the *inherent* value of cultural diversity. Contrast, for instance, Reith's rhetoric from 1924 with these statements from a BBC policy document published in 2011 – called, tellingly, 'Everyone Has a Story':

> Quite simply, our determination to visibly increase our diversity on and off air is part of our fundamental commitment to serve all our audiences ... . Reflecting diversity through who we are and what we do is core to achieving those ambitions, enabling us to share stories that offer something to everyone in our audience, and that reflect our audience's diverse experiences in an authentic and credible way. Everyone is different and everyone has a story.
>
> (BBC, 2011b)

Broadcasting, the document makes clear, serves an audience by reflecting its culture back to itself as accurately as possible. In a culturally diverse society, this means a culturally diverse output. Clearly, the BBC's not going as far as to say that minority cultures are to be celebrated more than majority ones. But, equally clearly, simply being a culture of some kind has become, as Eagleton puts it, 'of value in itself' (2000: 14). And, implicitly at least, a public service broadcaster such as the BBC nowadays asserts that 'authentic' culture is something we're supposed to approve of rather than change.

It's hard to dispute this narrative as a broad-brush outline: the evidence of change is unequivocally there in the programmes as well as the policy documents. It's hard, too, not to see the fair-minded inclusiveness of the present-day BBC as a marker of genuine progress. But, as I hope to show in this chapter, there are, nevertheless, difficulties thrown up by such a narrative.

Three in particular arise. One is that in conceiving of culture as affirming a specific identity – rather than affirming something universal and timeless – we are still left with the problem of social conflict, since, as Eagleton suggests, even subcultures sometimes create 'pluralized conformism' or a 'blind particularism': 'unified by their antagonism to others, they can succeed in transposing into local terms the global closure they detest in the classical notion of culture' (2000: 42). Some experiences and truths – pain, suffering, love, justice – are surely still universal, and we might reasonably expect public service broadcasting to acknowledge that. A second difficulty with our narrative is that it depends on exaggerating the cultural elitism of institutions such as the BBC, especially in its early days. A more nuanced history of the period might challenge this. The third difficulty is that our narrative offers a false dichotomy between 'high' and 'popular' culture or between culture as aesthetics and culture as way-of-life. In truth, all cultures are involved in one another. Even for a conservative Christian like T. S. Eliot, the different versions of culture were not mutually exclusive. One of the original meanings of culture is 'husbandry' – the tendency of natural growth. So culture is about an *activity* as much as an *entity*. It's about the *working* of one culture on another.

This 'enriching' through husbandry – *cultivation*, essentially – comes close to describing the conceptual framework within which we might best understand the cultural role of public service broadcasting. Perhaps this is unsurprising, given that the original meaning of the word 'broadcasting' lies in an agricultural metaphor: a scattering of seeds. But, in fact, institutions such as the BBC, even in Reith's day, were even more radically democratic in the scale of their ambitions than this might imply. Eliot wanted to enrich popular culture, but he lacked faith in people's ability to understand or appreciate good art or literature in its own terms. Which is why, for Eliot, there needed to be a priest-like caste to skilfully convert true art into something a bit more palatable and intuitive – rather as organized religion converts abstract theology into daily rituals and observances to be practised by everyday believers almost as a matter of habit. Now on the face of it, this sounds remarkably like the role assumed by public broadcasters – entailing, as it does, the daily work of translating 'difficult' material into 'accessible' programmes. But that's only ever been part of their offering. A glance at the schedules of public broadcasters across the world shows that they frequently choose *not* to translate or simplify. Sometimes they give us *direct* experiences – transmitting, say, live coverage of music or unexpurgated book readings or full-length productions of Shakespeare or Aeschylus. More importantly, even in mainstream output there is at the heart of public service broadcasting an inherent faith that almost every one of us *is* capable of growth. The task is not – and has never been – one of tilling empty soil: it's one of working over and fertilizing what's already there. The senior BBC producer Huw Wheldon once described the task memorably: public service broadcasting was not just about 'making the good popular'; it was also about making 'the popular good'. Much of this two-way engagement, I would argue, survives. Perhaps not everywhere, and perhaps especially not in rampantly commercial media environments. But often enough in the schedules of public service broadcasters to justify their persistent claim to have a special cultural role in the modern world.

From Laboratory to Corridor

One aspect of public service broadcasting's engagement with culture that is often underplayed is its *own* creative activity. In other words, those moments where broadcasters don't so much mediate *other* works of culture as try to produce something from scratch themselves, as if broadcasting is *itself* a kind of art rather than a conveyor belt for the established arts of, say, literature, theatre, music, painting or film. There is a rich history of this 'culture-creating' tradition, stretching from pioneering radio features in the 1920s through to epic drama serials or highly stylized television documentaries in the twenty-first century. But it's not been a universally *celebrated* tradition. Its proponents have seen broadcasting as something qualitatively new, and thus ripe for original and experimental work. Its detractors, suspicious of what smacks of self-indulgence, think of broadcasting as something demanding self-effacement – where letting pre-existing work reach its audience with as little interference as possible is the true cultural service on offer. We might, then, see the former group as conceiving broadcasting to be a kind of laboratory – a creative space; and the latter as conceiving broadcasting to be more of a corridor – a consciously characterless but highly effective passageway through which other stuff might move freely. The public service ethos is capacious enough to embrace both conceptions.

The original impulse to conceive of broadcasting as a new and exciting laboratory certainly made sense. In its very earliest days, radio sometimes consisted of little more than a few people standing before a microphone reading aloud some short book extracts or news articles from the papers, or maybe performing scenes from plays or brief musical skits. Even when radio was adventurous enough to attempt 'relays' of stage plays or full-scale music concerts, the medium's role was really just to eavesdrop on something that was happening anyway. But, as LeMahieu argues, in an organization such as the BBC, many staff knew that they would only gain credibility among respectable folk if their work could be seen as being aesthetically superior to 'mass' commercial enterprises, such as cinema, newspapers or music hall (1988: 178–9). This meant foregrounding their own interventions in the communicative act.

One strategy was to keep highlighting radio's unique contribution in fostering a new age of orality. Magazine articles or speeches by broadcasters frequently extolled the virtues of the spoken word as having a cultural power that surpassed that of the written word, while leading poets were encouraged to see in radio the means of reviving the 'lost' oral traditions of their own art. W. B. Yeats, for instance, had long thought of poetry in 'Bardic' terms – as an inherently public act where one chanted lines in a musical fashion in the pub or on the stage or street corner. In the early 1930s, when he'd rather lost confidence in this dream, Yeats was cajoled into performing on the BBC. Reaching vast audiences was, he imagined, a chance to 'recover through radio the "Homeric Dream"', and, excited by the experience, he quickly predicted that 'broadcasting may change the oratory of the world' (Schuchard, 2008: 335). He was getting a little carried away. But the very act of broadcasting clearly worked some sort of magic: Yeats believed that it was through radio that he'd 'recovered' the power of his youth and was able to produce a fresh wave of ballads and verses (376–80). According to the American poet Archibald MacLeish, writing in 1938, Yeats – and the BBC – had together helped poetry 're-enter the world' for the first time in a century (398). Whether exaggerated or not, this was a signifi-cant claim: that broadcasting could shift wholesale the nature of cultural life by its very presence.

A second strategy for establishing broadcasting's own cultural credentials was more daring: it was to use the technology of radio to create a new 'art of sound'. In Germany a thriving radio avant-garde existed in the 1920s and early 1930s. In various regional stations, producers such as Hans Flesch, Friedrich Bischoff, Friedrich Wolf and Walter Ruttmann would record sounds optically onto film stock and then cut and splice them, to play with the textures of radio and 'capture and rearrange' the sounds of 'daily experience'. In so doing, a completely new genre was created: the 'acoustical film' (Gilfillan, 2009: 3). The equivalent for British listeners was the live 'multi-studio' technique used by producers such as Lance Sieveking in programmes like *Kaleidoscope* (1928), which melded together performances taking place simultaneously in different rooms so that listeners heard a collage of dramatic scenes and poems mixed with classical music or jazz, all inter-spersed with sound-effects. Like his German contemporaries, he was trying to do with *time* what film directors had done with *space* – namely, to fracture perspective and chronology through dramatic switches between 'close-up' and 'long shot', through sudden changes of scene and so on. Indeed, for Sieveking the 'mosaic' quality he thus achieved – 'this kaleidoscope of action' – was '*the* radio of radio' (Sieveking, 1935: 25–6). Jump forward forty years and we find similar experiments being conducted by another BBC producer, Michael Mason. He collaborated extensively with the Radiophonic Workshop – a true laboratory in one small corner of the BBC, set up in 1958 to play around with tape-loops, multi-track machines and the first synthesizers. The result, in his case, was another series of epic, richly layered montage features, starting with *A Bayeux Tapestry* and *Rus* in the late 1960s and ending with *Sunken Treasure* in 1983. Again, the aim was to create a series of sensations rather than a traditional narrative, and in this he succeeded magnificently. While Sieveking had described his work as 'painting in sound', Mason called his own programmes 'audiophonies' (Hendy, 2007). None of this laboratory work was particularly easy on the ear – or even intended to be. Indeed, many listeners clearly found it incomprehensible. In terms of leading listeners gently and carefully towards an appreciation of the more demanding cultural products of the age, the BBC's modernist extravaganzas clearly stretched the public's patience to breaking point. Nevertheless, the desire of producers such as Sieveking or Mason to reach as many people as possible was real enough. And even if their programmes only ever appealed to a select few, they stimulated *others* in broadcasting to work in a more adventurous spirit. Douglas Kahn, in a study of the avant-garde, suggests that 'misguided aspirations, the oddest of infatuations, failed attempts' have often been 'more provocative than complete, final, and flawless realizations' (Kahn, 1992: 1–3). At the BBC, Sieveking's value was that in welding words together with music and sound in what he wanted to be an equal partnership he had established within the BBC a model of radio with a more textured aural quality, where 'every moment of experience could be grist to the microphone' (Fielden, 1960: 110). In short, he'd shown the way to what would later be called the 'radio feature' – a small but distinguished broadcasting genre that's since been exported around the world. In the late 1960s, Mason's audiophonies, though testing the BBC's technical resources to the limit, also prompted others at the BBC to think on a larger scale or to extend the possibilities of stereo and multi-track mixing. Such 'laboratory' work, protected from the demand for quick returns, was the broadcasting equivalent of speculative or 'pure' science: if tolerated and given time and space to mature, it led to innovation percolating gently and unobtrusively through the whole sector.

We might not expect to see this kind of risky experimentation in television, which, as a medium is not just more expensive to make than radio but always more attuned to the demands of the 'mainstream' audience. But actually there *are* plentiful examples of programmes which, arguably, represent collectively the creation of a genuinely new cultural form. Hence, if we glance backwards across the past sixty years or so, we see 'television drama', rather as radio had done before it, emerge slowly from a period in the late 1940s and early 1950s characterized by the transmission of live studio dramas barely distinguishable from theatre performances, into a more confidently visual – indeed, filmic – style, with the ability to record and edit allowing greater freedom in terms of plot and texture (see Cooke, 2003). This wasn't simply a case of a stage aesthetic being swapped for a cinema aesthetic. Something distinctively televisual was being forged at each stage. For example – and to name just one celebrated example out of many – an early American television drama such as *Marty* (1953) had both the spontaneity of liveness which cinema lacked and the ability to get right up close to its characters which the stage lacked. In combining these two effects, then adding a third – an ability, like radio, to reach instantaneously into millions of homes – the *New York Times'* critic Jack Gould reckoned *Marty* had created a new Holy Trinity in modern aesthetics (Gould, 2002). In later years, as Kristin Thompson has shown, television grew into itself in other ways: it typically developed as a serial form – and has thus become more open-ended, with a greater opportunity for complexity and layering, and a greater focus on character and community than that achieved in the cinema (Thompson, 2003).

The extent to which television's now entitled to make great cultural claims for itself *as television* can be seen in the critical reaction to one of most celebrated drama serials of recent years – *The Wire* (2002–8). Each of its five series focused on a different aspect of Baltimore's war against drugs – policing, schooling, politics and so on. But it took sixty episodes for the overarching narrative arc to unfold – a narrative in which the city

> is not just a stand-in for Western civilization or globalized urban rot or the American inner city now given the cold federal shoulder in the folly-filled war on terror ... [it] is also just plain itself, with a very specific cast of characters, dead and alive.
>
> (Moore, 2010)

In other words, it is a drama showing how television can be both epic *and* intimate. Indeed, so 'rich and roaming', so soaked in verisimilitude is it, that its main writer, David Simon has often referred to it, not as 'television' but as a 'novel' – in an implicit rebuke to the medium as a whole. But this is rhetorical. And as far as one novelist is concerned, *The Wire* undoubtedly qualifies as the 'premier example of a new art form' (Moore, 2010).

The Wire, of course, like its distant progenitor, *Marty*, is a product of American *commercial* television – the former on Home Box Office (HBO), the latter on NBC. This presents us with a problem. For any success in the commercial sector surely makes it harder to see what the distinctive contribution of *public service* broadcasting has been to the establishment of television drama as an innovative cultural form. This hasn't gone unnoticed by some cultural commentators, especially on the pro-market right. One of the British Conservative Party's main advisors on media policy, David Elstein, for example, suggests that the success of HBO in particular 'challenges a traditional core defence of public service broadcasting: that only public subsidy through an institution like the BBC can ensure intelligent, accessible quality drama, which the market would otherwise fail to deliver to our screens' (Elstein, 2010, opendemocracy.net). But, as the example of Grace Wyndham Goldie and her team of young current affairs staff showed in Chapter 2, it is in the BBC that creativity has more often than not found a foothold. So, in the history of drama we can point to the example of Rudolph Cartier, the Austrian émigré cinematographer recruited by the BBC in 1952. According to Lez Cooke, Cartier was 'given the opportunity and the freedom to shake up BBC television drama', creating at least two landmark programmes that predate the start of commercial television in Britain: *The Quatermass Experiment* (1953) and *Nineteen Eighty-Four* (1954) (Cooke, 2003: 20–8). Later examples of innovative work incubated within the protective environment of the BBC include those by a cohort of young directors recruited in the 1960s, including Ken Loach, Stephen Frears and Roland Joffe, who were given the freedom to dispense with detailed scripts and dialogue, take their cameras out and about and work for long hours in their editing suites, in order to construct less writerly, more visual television plays. More recently, there is the example of the 'documentarist' Adam Curtis, technically just another producer working in BBC current affairs, but someone whose 'originality and gifts have earned him a privileged position as an in-house video philosopher and archive-crawler' (*Sunday Times*, 22 May 2011). Operating his own camera and sound-recording equipment, he's also allowed to be his own editor and narrator. The result – series such as *The Power of Nightmares* (2004) and *All Watched Over by Machines of Loving Grace* (2011) – is television that is topical and opinionated but also richly layered, visually, aurally and metaphorically; television, in fact, which defies easy description.

We can, then, see public service broadcasting repeatedly allowing talented individuals the creative time and space to practise their craft, try new techniques, take risks. Often, this investment has resulted in audiences being given something they did not ask for, but which later turned out to be hugely popular or at least possess cult appeal. It is true that commercial broadcasting has nurtured laboratory work of this kind. Cooke and others have traced for us a history of creative drama in British commercial television to match that in America – from *Armchair Theatre* in the 1950s through to a flurry of socially aware real-life dramas in the 1990s, such as *Who Bombed Birmingham?* (1990), *Hillsborough* (1997) and *The Murder of Stephen Lawrence* (1999). But the narrative also shows that over time the logic of commercial funding – the need, crudely, to maximize ratings and minimize costs – has been progressively squeezing out room on the schedules for experimental or challenging drama. In a market-regulated environment it is a logic that applies to mainstream public service broadcasters as well as commercial ones. But it doesn't usually apply equally. As Barnett and Seymour show through their content analysis of British television in the 1990s, the tendency towards 'predictable' formats, soap operas and 'star names', and the consequent lack of opportunity for new talent and new styles, is at its strongest wherever the overriding priority is 'to get very big ratings' – or, as industry executives put it, wherever we have 'caution brought on by commercial pressure' (1999: 69, 51–2). In the circumstances, a public sector – which asserts that ratings are not the *only* factor that needs to be taken into account – will tend to be better placed to nurture experiment, even if only on a modest scale.

Indeed, for public service broadcasters it all comes down to a precarious balancing act: the need to show cultural leadership – to be, as it were, in advance of public taste – and the equally powerful need to ensure audience figures don't fall below a critical level by being *too far* in advance of the public. In other words, to be reflective of the full range of popular as well as minority tastes. It's this balancing act that means an organization such as the BBC, though keen to nurture wayward talent and take risks, does so only within firm limits. Moreover, there is the persistent pursuit of that old BBC injunction mentioned earlier – 'to make the good popular and the popular good'. In this respect, there's a telling statistic from 2008. When it was on the subscription-only channel HBO that year, the final season of *The Wire* secured an audience of just 1 million American viewers – out of a national population of some 300 million. When it was shown in Britain late at night on BBC2, it achieved almost the same audience figure – but out of a national population *one-fifth the size* (*Daily Telegraph*, 2 April 2009). *The Wire's* re-broadcast on the BBC, then, was perhaps even more significant than its original transmission on HBO. Making a hard-hitting drama about Baltimore drug culture that's been likened to Aeschylus, Balzac and Shakespeare available to *every* citizen was the bolder act of public service.

But, to reiterate: delivering the 'ground-breaking' piece of 'pure' radio or television is only a small part of the public service broadcaster's cultural remit. And there have always been highly articulate arguments, coming from within the sector, which are defiantly suspicious of the 'laboratory' model. The fundamental objection has been that it can sometimes come across as being in the service of the producer rather than the consumer. As one of the German pioneers put it, 'the insertion of the machine in the mediation process' threatened to displace that even more important cultural service to the public: for broadcasting to be not a creator but 'a guide' to art (Gilfillan, 2009: 64–5).

Overall, it's been this role as cultural *guide* that dominates the workaday world of public service. And even when the guidance provided is of the most uninvolved kind – when we have radio and television acting as a mere conveyor belt of 'other' stuff – it should not be dismissed lightly. Indeed, it might even represent best practice. Take, for instance, the experience of the novelist Jonathan Raban. He gets his inspiration, he once said, not from listening intently to the dramatic productions of Beckett, Pinter or Stoppard, but from soaking up the steady flow of all the other broadcasting output – the music, the chat shows, the stream of news bulletins. None of this offers 'very much in the way of a formal tradition', he said. But it's 'a corridor through which the whole world passes' – something 'chaotically eclectic ... by turns gossipy, authoritative, preachy, natural, artificial, confidential, loudly public, and not infrequently wordless'. As such, it represents 'an enormous, bottomless reservoir of conventions and techniques' in which he can fish endlessly for ideas and provocations. It sustains *his* art, he says. And, by implication, the same kind of 'ordinary' stuff sustains us all (Raban, 1981: 78–90).

From Hierarchies to Horizons

One implication of Raban's words is that broadcasting's sheer variety is its most important cultural facet. But have public service broadcasters always delivered variety? In his day, Reith had wanted the BBC to offer largely the canon of literature, music and art, and he had assumed that 'the best' of culture was generally to be found in London. This had meant a highly centralized regime, with Head Office always very much in charge (Scannell, 2000: 57; Reith, 1924: 63–72). British music was automatically equated with English music, and deep-rooted musical traditions in Wales, Scotland and Ireland were marginalized, just as regional traditions within England itself were persistently overlooked (Scannell and Cardiff, 1991: 303). American culture, which was beginning to make its presence felt through the new dance crazes, jazz music, movies and cocktail parties that helped define the 'Roaring Twenties', clearly needed to be kept at arm's length, too, for American culture bespoke a more open society that implied, rather unhelpfully, that 'one person's views and values were as good as another's' (299). In the BBC's view at this time, Britain had to remain the 'non-America' (Camporesi, 2000: 197). Reith's prejudices were hardly unusual. Conservatives welcomed any reassertion of tradition; progressives welcomed any bulwark against rampant commercialism. There was a wide consensus in favour of cultural orthodoxy – especially among the middle class. Cinema, books and the stage were all heavily regulated and highly censored. The BBC was, if anything, more liberal than most national institutions in this regard. Even so, broadcasting then 'reflected the biases and most treasured cultural aspirations' of the upper middle classes (LeMahieu, 1988: 83). When the BBC discussed the culture of Britain's 'Industrial North' in its annual 'Handbook' of 1928, it was by reference to just two local institutions: the Hallé Orchestra and the *Manchester Guardian* (147). No wonder so many people felt the BBC was aloof, unfriendly and patronizing. This was hardly a national institution reaching deeply into the subsoil of its community.

But, of course, from the BBC's point of view, there seemed little point in such digging. What most working-class people were interested in doing during their precious hours of leisure was, evidently, going to the pictures to see the latest Hollywood film, dancing at the local palais, drinking at the pub, watching a football match or even staying home to read a popular romance or two (see McKibbin, 1998). It wasn't just that none of this yet registered as culture. It was that the whole mission of broadcasting was surely to introduce such people to the glories of culture about which they were, sadly, ignorant. To have reflected 'authentic' working-class life would have been to 'level down' – when what was wanted was *up*lift. After all, the stated mission was not just to change individuals but to make 'sweetness and light' prevail: instead of *satisfying* public demand, it was all about *changing* it through the tight control of supply. To put it in the BBC's own terms, the intention was that we could grow to like that upon which we are fed.

If this seems a forbidding and elitist attitude, we need to acknowledge that from the start, broadcasters have deployed a number of strategies in an attempt to bring the audience along willingly on this journey to the cultural uplands, rather than having to drag it reluctantly. One strategy has been to accompany 'difficult' programmes with helpful explanation. In the early days, for example, evangelists for music, such as Sir Walford Davies, were put on air to help explain the meaning of music from the likes of Beethoven and other great composers in series such as *Music and the Ordinary Listener* (1926). Knowledgeable but never opinionated, Davies could bridge that troubling gap between 'expert' and 'layman' (Briggs, 1995, v.1: 259). A second strategy was embedded in the famed 'mixed' scheduling of the BBC, which ensured that listeners tuning in for something 'easy' on the ear or eye – say, some light dance music – would then be exposed, almost before they knew it, to something rather more difficult which they had not been seeking: a strategy of education by stealth. A third approach was to leaven the schedules with a large dose of middling fare – in the case of music, perhaps 'light orchestral' tunes – which would act as a kind of inoffensive buffer-zone between 'highbrow' and 'lowbrow' tastes (Scannell and Cardiff, 1991: 214). On the face of it, all these 'first stage' strategies were undermined when, in 1946, the BBC reorganized its programming into a 'pyramid' of three separate networks, apparently reinforcing rather than challenging old cultural hierarchies. At the bottom, the Light Programme would bring undemanding pleasure to the largest part of the British audience; in the next layer up, the Home Service would bring a residual mix of music and speech to the broad middle; then, at the pinnacle, the Third Programme would offer undiluted highbrow culture – and, specifically, an unexpurgated classical repertoire – to the most discerning minority. True to his original vision, Reith – who had by then left the BBC – found the new model 'objectionable' precisely because it ring-fenced culture for a tiny minority, rather than diffusing it in the generality of the BBC's services (Carpenter, 1996: 110).

Even with this pyramid, however, the BBC's underlying conception of its audience remained dynamic. One little-noticed feature of the model was that the three layers were designed to overlap a little in terms of programming – so there were plenty of 'crossing-points' rather than rigidly policed borders. The hope was that over time, people would move up through the pyramid, and, eventually, it would be inverted – the majority of people coming to like 'the best' rather than the 'worst'. This was certainly naïve. But at least it showed an enduring faith in human nature. And, it should be added, the BBC was not alone in putting its faith in this dynamic approach. As Goodman shows, the 'civic paradigm' among some American broadcasters ensured, for instance, that there was a significant amount of classical music on mainstream commercial stations in the US through the 1930s and 1940s (2011: 35). As in Britain, there were insistent claims about classical music's 'universal' value and appeal. It was 'civilizing', not just because it represented one of the pinnacles of Western artistic achievement, but because it was capable of instilling in individuals cosmopolitanism, emotional control, sensitivity, even feelings of kinship: part of its importance was its *transformative* nature. Indeed, the stronger the belief in its redemptive or improving powers, 'the more compelling was the case for wanting larger numbers of people to share in them' (118).

One important test of all this cultural manoeuvring by the broadcasters is surely the degree of success it had – or didn't have – in actually changing the cultural life of a nation. Goodman himself is in little doubt that the 'almost constant availability' of the classical repertoire ensured 'the generation of Americans that grew up with radio in the 1930s and 1940s developed and retained a love of classical music unmatched by those that followed them' (118). In a 1938 poll, for example, as many as 62.5 per cent of those questioned said they liked to listen to classical music on the radio (140). In Britain, there's evidence that the sum total of musical activity and interest increased as a result of the BBC efforts. In the 'land without music', the broadcaster's patronage of classical music, for example, boosted employment opportunities for orchestral musicians, and stimulated public interest in choral singing and concert-going (Briggs, 1995, v.1: 230). Overall, McKibbin suggests, the classical repertoire and the British 'musical imagination' were expanded by the Corporation's persistent willingness to pursue that vital, decisive and far-reaching invocation of Reith's – to 'give the public slightly better than it now thinks it likes' (1998: 460, 473–4).

We also need to dispel a long-standing misconception about the BBC and its historical belief in a hierarchy of cultural value. Undoubtedly, as an institution it found it immensely difficult to approach working men and women without condescension, or to assimilate the features of their lives into its programmes. Yet, even at the height of Reithian zeal, it was never simply force-feeding an undiluted diet of forbidding and alien fare onto a reluctant population. Producers and managers had ways of taking the temperature of audience reaction: letters in their postbag or in the *Radio Times*, comments in newspapers and so on. Even Reith acknowledged that the 'social centre of gravity' among listeners was, as he put it, 'much nearer the bottom than the top of the social scale', and that programming needed to take this into account (McIntyre, 1993: 174). Indeed, he was explicit on the need to give pleasure as well as edification:

> I do not in any way imply that merit is to be found exclusively in the classics of music or literature, or that transmissions of this nature are the only ones in which the broadcaster is really interested or the only ones which he feels are worth doing, If this were his view ... it would indicate an entire misconception of his function. It is most important that light and 'entertaining' items be sent out. The broadcaster puts as much energy and care into work of this nature, which shall constitute a pleasing relaxation after a hard day's work, as into items which tend to edification and wider knowledge.
>
> (Reith, 1924: 133–4)

So it is important to note the precise balance of programming on the BBC in these early years. 'Talks' amounted to less than a quarter of output; religious programmes about 2 per cent; drama just over 3 per cent; early music or modernist compositions amounted to less than one-tenth of 1 per cent; and classical music in general came to less than 10 per cent. In contrast, 'popular' music and 'dance music' together accounted for more than 35 per cent of output and light orchestral music another 12 (Briggs, 1995, v.1: 229; 357). There was, in other words, a decisive bias in favour of popular material *almost from the beginning*. Reith's underlying principle in shaping output was, after all, to ensure that 'for the greatest period the greatest number may be satisfied' (Reith, 1924: 122). This deeper history is important because it shows that it wasn't just the arrival of commercial TV in 1955 that suddenly forced a reluctant and inflexible BBC from an 'elite' cultural policy to a more inclusive one. The arrival of a brasher, slicker, more populist competitor certainly encouraged the BBC – but only into moving faster along a route it was already taking. It had always evolved – of necessity, since it always had to retain the national audience that gave it legitimacy as a national instrument of broadcasting.

Whether public service broadcasters such as the BBC have been *intrinsically* ill adapted to the informality, diversity and lack of deference which has characterized the post-Second World War cultural landscape is another question. After all, a long-standing institution with embedded routines and practices will surely always be carrying too heavy a weight of tradition or be too 'corporate' in manner to respond appropriately to rapid social change. And an institution which had originally conceived of culture as a universal force capable of playing down social divisions would surely be hopeless when it came to reflecting a more pluralist and dissonant world. Indeed, despite the arrival of commercial television and commercial radio between the 1950s and the early 1970s, there was, as Sylvia Harvey argues (2003: 52), a 'slowly surfacing public dissatisfaction with the blandness, "safeness" and establishment partiality' of British broadcasting. By the mid-1970s, almost everyone was agreed that, culturally speaking, the centre could not hold. A public broadcasting system founded on the earlier Reithian notion of 'a coherent if stratified society imbued with a certain sense of mutual obligation and a consensual idea of cultural and artistic value which emanated from its elite' had to be replaced by one which 'posited a more heterogeneous society ... each of whose elements had its own view of the world and its own concept of what was culturally significant' (Crisell, 2002: 202). Though the word 'multiculturalism' was not yet in wide circulation, its moment had arrived.

The most obvious means of ensuring that broadcasting reflected this moment was to create a completely new television sector with a completely new ethos. This was therefore one of the key recommendations of the British government-appointed Annan Committee when it reported in 1977. The plan was that a new channel would ensure diversity on air by being, not a programme-maker itself, but a commissioner and 'publisher' of programmes made by others. It would also be funded by a variety of sources – including rival cultural bodies such as the Arts Council. And it would be supervised by a new, and suggestively titled 'Open Broadcasting Authority' (203–4). This radical, if somewhat bureaucratic blueprint changed when the Conservatives came to power in 1979: the new channel was placed instead under the supervision of the body responsible for commercial TV, namely the Independent Broadcasting Authority (IBA). Even so, much of the original thinking survived. And when Channel 4 was launched in 1982, it represented a new variant of the public service model. First, it was a wholly owned subsidiary of the IBA, without private investors seeking a profit and funded by subventions from regional ITV companies rather than having to raise its revenue directly from advertising. There was thus a kind of editorial buffer-zone which broke the iron link that had hitherto existed 'between the quality, or even existence, of programmes and the size or value of their audiences' (207). This enabled Channel 4 to screen special-interest programmes without worrying about ratings. Second, many of its programmes were supplied by new, small-scale independent production companies. It was hoped this, too, would not only create a new 'cottage industry' in broadcast production but also allow a wider range of sensibilities and voices to make their way onto British television screens. As we shall see in Chapter 5, this ambition wasn't always sustained. But for several years at least there was every sign of genuine novelty. *The Eleventh Hour* (1994–6), for example, broadcast anti-government and avant-garde material late at night; *Comment* (1985) gave 'ordinary' people and campaigners the chance to present an opinionated take on the day's news; and a range of new documentaries and chatshows such as *Asian Eye* (1993–) and *Black on Black* (1983–5) covered issues of interest to ethnic minorities or presented a distinctively internationalist approach to current affairs. In Wales, meanwhile, viewers were provided with S4C, the first completely separate Welsh-language television channel (52–3; Ellis, 2003: 96). It is possible to see in all this a 'crucible' where programme-makers 'haltingly learned how to address niche or targeted audiences rather than use the universalising forms of address developed for a mass audience' (Ellis, 2003: 96).

The attempt to reconfigure public service broadcasting for the multicultural era wasn't just a British phenomenon, of course. Nor was it restricted to one moment in the 1970s. In Canada and across much of Europe, for instance, thousands of community broadcasting initiatives stretch back over the past four decades, each built on the idea that sheer localness and a do-it-yourself approach to production provided the best guarantees that diversity could be properly reflected. In Berlin, the reaction against 'universalising forms of address' reached its zenith in 1994 in the form of Radio Multikulti: a station offering no overarching 'tone' but, instead, a rich mosaic of programmes, each targeted at one of the many migrant communities in the city. In America there have been several attempts to reach down into the nation's subcultures through some sort of organized public system ever since the first Pacifica radio stations opened in the 1940s. The hesitant launch of public television in the 1950s and the more decisive launch of National Public Radio at the end of the 1960s were both attempts to counter what had been characterized as 'a vast wasteland' of bland network television programming targeted at the middle-class family audiences – not to mention a depressing vista of predictable, formatted-to-death commercial radio stations. As NPR's mission statement put it, the aim was to 'encourage a sense of active, constructive participation rather than apathetic helplessness' (Ledbetter, 1997: 117). By the 1980s, however, the rather middle-class feel of NPR suggested to some observers that *its* 'alternative' identity had long since been discarded 'like an outgrown cocoon' (130). Similarly, city television stations previously supported by the Corporation for Public Broadcasting had been forced to call on corporate sponsors and, with more conservative programmes, had become 'increasingly associated with a sense of effete cultural snobbery' (Marcus, 2003: 56). Indeed, stations often found the very label 'public' was enough to stop ethnic minority groups tuning in: it seemed to scream out loud that it just wasn't 'for them' (Malatia, 2007: 20). Conscious of this monocultural reputation, public TV and radio stations across the US have steadily woven into their schedules more and more 'specialist' programmes targeted at, say, African-Americans, Latinos or Asian-Americans – or, as in Britain, taken their programmes from a wider variety of production companies.

The result of all this is that when it comes to culture, any notion of there being some sort of unifying 'identity' to public service broadcasting is now remarkably elusive. By 2007 one station manifesto went so far as to declare that there was 'no such entity' as 'the public radio system'. 'As a collective of independent radio stations, we share our common New Deal birth', it said, 'but little else': 'We must be individual, because we serve communities that are individual' (20–1). It was almost as if the whole notion of a collective 'public' had been written out of the script.

Cultivation

Even for the most established public service broadcasters, the implications of this more democratic version of culture have been far-reaching. In Britain, for example, Channel 4's use of independent production companies immediately increased the pressure on *all* broadcasters, including the BBC, to make fewer programmes in-house: diversity behind the scenes came to be regarded as a necessary first step in ensuring diversity on air. At a more philosophical level, the Annan Report had also implied that it was no longer the role of broadcasters to 'set themselves up as social engineers'. Once upon a time, it was suggested, broadcasters such as the BBC had actively encouraged audiences towards experiencing a whole range of programmes. Now, the thinking went, their duty was simply to offer a menu featuring 'as many tastes and interests as possible' and then adopt a position of cultural indifference. How far viewers or listeners pursued the full range of output was entirely a matter for them (Crisell, 2002: 203).

As it happens, the whole notion of pushing people towards something they might not choose for themselves wasn't just philosophically unfashionable: it was becoming practically impossible, too. Over the past four decades, alongside the multiplication of cultural representations there's been a multiplication in the number of 'narrowcast' channels – channels that give audiences the kind of television or radio viewers or listeners want to the exclusion of everything else. For television the examples are well known: non-stop sport on Sky, non-stop music on MTV, wildlife documentaries on National Geographic and so on. In her study of American radio, Susan Douglas points to much the same happening with highly formatted music stations. These are places where, as she puts it, 'variety is kept outside the door'. Promotional ads assure listeners that 'they won't ever have to hear heavy metal, rap, or anything unexpected'. They get 'safe, gated-in listening' in a world of 'mutually exclusive auditory niches' (Douglas, 1999: 348–9). This, Douglas says, contrasts with an earlier period of cultural openness and exchange. In the 1930s or 1950s, for instance, the eclectic mix of music on any given station meant, say, suburban white teenagers got the chance to listen to African-American jazz or blues: in other words, there was playful, unpredictable listening in a world of mutually overlapping auditory cultures. At the level of the individual listener, she concludes, the loss of this cultural openness represents a narrowing of personal horizons; at the national scale, it represents a tragic decline in the 'American imagination'.

Public service broadcasters have followed this trend and, simultaneously, also attempted to stand outside it. Thus, in the case of the BBC, some television channels clearly have a 'narrowcast' element: BBC3 is generally orientated towards younger viewers; BBC News provides near-continuous news; BBC Parliament covers in depth the proceedings of the House of Commons and House of Lords. Similarly, in radio, the BBC's national networks have been organized along 'generic' lines since the late 1960s: Radio 1 delivering pop and rock for younger listeners, Radio 2 classic rock and middle-of-the-road music for the broadly middle-aged; Radio 3 classical music; Radio 4 speech programmes; Radio 5 Live, sports and rolling news. Digitalization has taken this further, with even more specialist services such as the self-explanatory Asian Network, or 1Extra, which broadcasts urban music to younger, predominantly Black British listeners. Yet it is possible for the BBC to claim that it still serves the *whole* population, since although these individual radio and television channels each reflect very particular aspects of British cultural life, when taken together, they add up to a comprehensive service. To remove any one of them would thus instantly 'skew' the BBC's overall coverage, and mean it was something less than a 'national' broadcaster.

At the same time, the BBC has been careful to ensure its channels are never entirely watertight. For a start, there remain several prominent channels that are thoroughly 'mixed' in their output. BBC1, for instance, still supplies a mainstream national television audience with a wide range of programmes. On one sample day in 2011 – 16 August – its schedule included, for example, regular news programmes, a cookery show, some popular history, several dramas, a comedy, a reality-style documentary, children's programmes (including a news magazine for children), an investigation into junk food for babies and a documentary about the Swedish coastline. Equally diverse is Radio 4, which, although generically labelled a 'speech' service, interprets this to encompass not just news and debate, but also drama, book readings, comedy, documentaries, panel-games and a whole range of specialist programmes about history, food, science, religion, film and the arts in general. One significant, but often overlooked aspect of Radio 4's identity is that, formally, it has no 'target audience': according to the BBC, it's just aimed at all those with 'curious minds'.

Nor is Radio 4 quite the exception it might at first seem. Take its sister station Radio 1. At a superficial level, it might appear to be unequivocally devoted to pop and rock for a teenage and young adult audience: no different, in essence, to any number of commercial music stations targeting the same 'demographic'. Yet, once more, if we look at the schedule for a sample day in 2011 – again, 16 August – we find that as well as the regular DJ-led music shows there are two fifteen-minute news programmes, each drawing on the full resources of the BBC's journalists across the globe, and two programmes covering the Edinburgh Festival, including the broadcast of a late-night cabaret. Even the music on Radio 1 is more 'mixed' than we might suppose. Like many other stations, there's a rough distinction between 'mainstream' music in the daytime, and minority tastes – punk, Asian and desi beats, hip-hop, dubstep and so on – at night. Judged solely in terms of the overall range of 'pop' music broadcast, this means Radio 1 stands apart from its direct commercial rivals – playing a larger number of different tracks over the course of each week. There is also a stated commitment to broadcast 'new music first'. This is, admittedly, a vague slogan. But it is one that involves playing tracks by relatively unknown bands well before they've entered the charts. This contrasts with standard practice in commercial radio, which is to play tracks only after their popularity's been confirmed through their appearance in 'radio play' or sales charts. More than that, though, as I have argued elsewhere, Radio 1 has attempted since the mid-1990s to blur the traditional boundary – one might even call it the traditional hierarchy – between daytime 'pop' and nighttime specialist music (Hendy, 2000). In the early-evening period, for instance, music's been carefully scheduled to provide a long overlap between the two sides of the output, so that there's no clear 'switch-off' point. In this way, listeners can be drawn gently into listening to more 'demanding' material almost without noticing. Radio 1's also been keen to emphasize the musical expertise of its presenters – showing them to be trusted guides to the 'best' work in each genre. Having done this, it has then encouraged these nighttime specialists to recommend to their daytime colleagues any tracks they believe have the potential to 'crossover' into the mainstream. This tackles head-on what the station's Managing Editor called 'the isolation of success' – where relatively marginal music is forever trapped in the 'ghetto' of off-peak broadcasting hours (755).

The example of Radio 1's music policy allows us to glimpse the outlines of a more general phenomenon: public service broadcasters pursuing what we might call a *neo*-Reithian cultural agenda. Look at BBC3, and we see a television network that doesn't just entertain its youth audience: it exposes it to programmes which it might otherwise not seek for itself, such as documentaries about the war in Afghanistan or series about what it's like to be a single parent. Tune into Vocalo 89.5, a public radio station serving Chicago and northwest Indiana, and we hear a station spurning the usual 'mosaic' approach of different shows for different ethnic groups – on the basis that that would direct its listeners' sensibilities 'into self-selected hallways' and reinforce the cultural segregation in society at large. Instead it offers 'a broadcast stream that integrates different points-of-view, cultures, interests, and ethnicities into the content, at all times' (Malatia, 2007: 23).

The echoes of Reith, who once complained that we too often 'take our pleasures in water-tight compartments', are striking (1924: 123). Now, as in the 1920s, we sense something of what Tracey calls 'the mighty and worthy ambition' of public service broadcasting: the idea that 'we can, collectively, be better than we are' (20). Being 'better', though, is no longer about a listener or viewer in an assumed state of *non*-culture having to learn about the 'right' sort of culture through the confident guidance of, say, the BBC. Nor are we being left entirely to our own devices, as the Annan Report assumed we should be back in 1977 – and as practised by the commercial system, with its orthodoxy of 'consumer sovereignty'. What we get instead is a commitment to cultural plurality combined with a continuing institutional effort to expand our horizons.

Public service broadcasting has dispensed with the notion of *vertical* cultivation – where a 'higher' culture enriches the lower reaches of society. But, at its most confident, it still attempts a kind of *horizontal* cultivation – where we viewers and listeners are enriched, through being quietly exposed to the fullest range of cultural experiences.

In the end, the contradiction between giving people what they *want* and giving them what they *need* turns out to be no contradiction at all. The BBC, in fact, has always done both. This is not conceptual confusion, so much as a twin-track strategy. And the contribution it makes to cultural life as a result of this approach is clear. It promotes 'the best' works of literature, drama, art and music – and makes them widely available. It tries to renew and develop culture, including the culture of broadcasting, by supporting innovation and experiment – but always with an eye to audience reaction. It is, as Seaton puts it, 'committed to catering for the diversity of the public, the enthusiasms of minorities, as well as of the majority ... to the breadth of public taste rather than its lowest common denominator'. In short, because it tries not to discriminate against any class or generation or ethnic group, it becomes a means to 'draw together society in its diversity' (Curran and Seaton, 1997: 335–6).

We sense, once again, the Enlightenment underpinnings of public service broadcasting – namely that radio and television can potentially help us all towards becoming rounded individuals, living lives of virtue and pleasure in equal parts. And pleasure really *is* just as important as rationality in this equation. David Brooks's *The Social Animal* (2011) stresses the importance of unconscious minds – saturated as they are with instincts, biases and habits – in silently shaping our most important attitudes. Brooks, in particular, suggests that public policy will always fail unless it takes into account the power of emotion to outweigh reason. He has a point. But his approach elevates emotion over reason, rather than seeing them as two intrinsically connected facets of humanity. Public service broadcasting operates on more balanced principles. It sees us, its audiences, as having emotional predispositions and prejudices, in culture as much as in politics; to that extent it indulges us – embracing cultural diversity and choice. Yet it assumes that we are also capable of transcending these predispositions and prejudices – in other words, that instincts can be worked over and changed, like fertile soil.

The concept of 'the public', then, remains absolutely central to public service broadcasting's cultural role. This concept is not, and never has been one in which people are regarded as listening or viewing passively – inert, empty, waiting to be filled up. As Briggs reminds us, even the patrician Reith treated the public with respect: 'not as nameless aggregates with statistically measurable preferences, or "targets" for the programme sponsor, but as living audiences capable of growth and development' (Briggs, 1995, v.1: 218). As I have tried to argue in this chapter, wherever mixed schedules survive – wherever there is, in fact, an effort to cultivate our minds with care and sensitivity rather than force and prejudice – that emancipatory ethos survives, too.

4 Service: The Ethos of the Broadcasters

In broadcasting, we are dealing with things made by living human beings. Programmes don't just fall off the end of a production line: there's a 'hidden labour' involved – production, that is, by thinking, feeling individuals (Scannell, 2007: 2–3). So it's important to ask at this point whether there is anything *distinctive* about the men and women who work in public service broadcasting. Specifically: are they fundamentally different to their commercial counterparts in terms of, say, character or ethos or professional attitude or creative ability? And even if they're not very different as individuals, might they operate *collectively*, within distinct working cultures or according to opposing sets of values?

Such questions are vital, since, despite any 'democratization' of the media through ever-wider access to the technology of programme-making, the power to decide what gets on the airwaves is still concentrated in relatively few hands. In national organizations such as the BBC, individual managers, commissioning editors and producers have immense influence over what large numbers of people see and hear. They represent, as some have put it, a 'New Priesthood', controlling the symbolic forms of the contemporary world in much the same way as, say, royal courts, universities or indeed the established churches did in previous ages (Garnham, 2000: 3). As the saying goes, power comes with responsibility. So can we trust these people to act wisely in this mediating process? Public service broadcasters face a multitude of pressures to be more competitive, more entrepreneurial, more efficient – in effect, to be more like their commercial counterparts. Yet, if they ever look like they are working in the service of vested interests – whether of capitalism, of government or a particular party or class – rather than in the service of the public at large, any right to a protected status would surely evaporate. Indeed, the argument for continuing to fund public service broadcasting must depend in part on a judgement of certain key people's performance. As Reith himself once said, the vocation 'goes up or down according to those who fill it' (1924: 35).

In attempting to explore this theme, we have to start by recognizing the continuing power of past practice in many public service institutions. People working there often see themselves as inheriting a particular professional aura that's accumulated over time. When the BBC began, for instance, Reith was clear that he only wanted staff who believed in the 'preservation of a high moral standard', whose underlying motive was that 'whatever is done shall be done well', who had 'imagination', who might come to be regarded by the public as 'guide, philosopher and friend', and who showed loyalty to the organization (32–53). The list of requirements was long and exacting. But Reith wasn't alone in setting the bar high. One of his successors, Hugh Carleton Greene, talked of BBC staff as a reserve of skilled people who needed to be 'honourable' (BBC, 1965: 8). Indeed, much the same language has been used by all Director-Generals right through to the present day. Some of this can be put down to corporate self-promotion. But there's also a practical reason for investing so much faith in the individual programme-maker: so vast is the output of a large organization such as the BBC that detailed oversight of day-to-day activity is impossible. In the last resort, it is the programme producer who determines the quality and tone of what goes out on air. Indeed, a fundamental feature of those who work in a public corporation such as the BBC is that they are afforded a great degree of freedom from managerial scrutiny or regulatory guidelines in their day-to-day work. Within certain parameters, they are trusted to 'get on with it' and exercise their own judgement.

The assumption that staff can operate without a tight and defined chain of command is generally based on the idea that they are united by an intuitive sense of common purpose. But this needs unpicking, for we need to be sure that an organization's *esprit de corps* isn't just another way of describing a closed and inward-looking mind-set. It is no accident, for instance, that some observers of the BBC have chosen to describe its employees – including even creative programme-makers at the sharp end of the machine – as 'officials' or 'administrators', or even 'functionaries' (Conolly, 2009: xiv; LeMahieu, 1988: 182–92). In some interpretations staff are viewed, in effect, as the operatives of a 'total institution of "media imperialism"' (Avery, 2006: 38). A more widely shared assumption is that these predominantly middle-class and highly educated people will – viewed from the Left – invariably represent 'establishment' thinking and values, or – viewed from the Right – consistently represent a progressive or permissive set of beliefs.

Perhaps, then, the central feature of the public broadcasters' working lives is their daily struggle between two fundamental interpretations of what it means to serve the public: between maintaining a broadcasting system that gives the public what it asks for and maintaining a broadcasting system that allows privileged individuals – that is, the broadcasters themselves – to decide things in advance *on the public's behalf.* It's a struggle that can be framed in lots of different ways: as a struggle, say, between reflecting public taste and shaping it; as a struggle between assuming that supply must follow demand and assuming that, on the contrary, demand can be shaped by supply; even as a struggle between the right of a creative artist to be true to his or her vision, whatever the cost, and the same artist's need to earn a regular wage and hold down a job. In 1975 a BBC Chairman once posed the dilemma in its most essential form: quite simply, he asked, is it the Corporation's role to lead or to follow? Reith, of course, would have been in no doubt that it was the former. But times change. By the 1970s it was already clear that, while the BBC might still seek to increase understanding or prefer 'truth to falsehood', it could never stand completely apart from the prevailing public mood. So, despite the weight of inherited tradition, we can't assume that what held in the 1920s still applies. Public service broadcasters work within a constantly changing political and social climate. And plenty of writers argue that a civil service ethos – or, more likely, a commercialized ethos – has now come to dominate, perhaps even to displace entirely, the old progressive slightly permissive and moderately bohemian instincts of an earlier era. The danger that public service broadcasters themselves cease being *sui generis* and become either clones of their commercial rivals or characterless 'operatives' in a self-sustaining bureaucracy with no vision of its ultimate purpose, can hardly be ignored.

Yet beneath the surface, certain distinctive values do endure. I hope to justify this claim over the following pages by exploring three key dimensions to the producer's role in public service broadcasting: first, 'professionalism' – the notion that the producer works to a set of standards; second, 'conscience' – the idea that the producer draws upon a set of 'internalized' values; and third, 'creativity' – the producer's struggle to maintain his or her sense of inventiveness in a large, and potentially stifling bureaucratic organization. In exploring these dimensions, I want to argue that it's precisely through the precarious day-by-day balancing of these contradictory pulls – and perhaps especially the pull between 'leading' and 'following' – that the broadcaster is transformed into an effective servant of the public.

Professionalism

Back in the 1920s, Reith asserted that if someone was being given the opportunity to broadcast to the entire population, that person needed to be 'of pre-eminent and recognized position' (1924: 148). And although Reith referred to those in front of the microphone rather than those working behind the scenes, there was no doubt then – or since – that the same kind of pre-eminence was required of the BBC's own back-room staff. Expertise within their chosen field, especially, has always been valued. George Fischer, a Senior Editor working at the BBC during the 1970s and 1980s, points out that the primary quality he sought from his producers was that they be 'authoritative' in their specialism. They needed, he says, to be capable of talking to scientists or artists or writers 'on equal terms'. 'To sit down with somebody – "I haven't read your book, but..." – that was totally out.' He tolerated mavericks, but only so long as they were 'high-flyers' capable of generating good ideas. If he had to define their job in its most essential terms, he says it was 'to find the best minds in the world, bring them to the microphone and turn them into ancient mariners' (interview, 2003): Fischer reckoned that it took one to know one. All this implied a high-status occupation. It's not surprising, therefore, to find personal accounts in which the prospect of working for the BBC is regarded as one of the plum jobs in British life. Take this, for example, from John Grist, another senior figure from the Fischer era, who'd joined the BBC's 'Talks' department two decades before:

> In the early 1950s the letters BBC were magic. It was still, and would be for many years, part of the deeply felt wartime experience of the British people ... . To go to work there was a feather in my cap ... . After I had been in the BBC about a year, I told my mother that I had been asked whether I would like to be put up to be a parliamentary candidate. She was quite shocked and said, 'Why would you want to go into Parliament when you have a job in the BBC?' ... A Talks Producer was a superior being. It was like being in the fast lane of the Civil Service ... . It put you into a special category, a higher plane than ordinary people.
>
> (Grist, 2004: 28–41)

For much of the Corporation's history, being a BBC producer has not only been accorded an elite status; it's also been given a distinctively intellectual character. Indeed, Nicholas Garnham argues that broadcasters constitute a 'New Priesthood' precisely because they are, in effect, full members of the intellectual 'class': along with newspaper and literary editors, policy-makers, gallery directors or writers, they have the power to define what is true, right and beautiful – and thus to represent a critical tradition appealing to universal values. They are therefore not just powerful, but, in the case of an organization such as the BBC, fully complicit in the grand 'project' of spreading Enlightenment values (2000: 83–6). Producers themselves might not use such grandiose terminology. But the implication of their language is much the same. John Grist, for example, says this:

> I took into the BBC an absolute belief in the idea of public service … . Implicit was the intention and the duty to uplift the quality of the lives of the audience by opening up the world to them.
>
> (Grist, 2004: 31)

If we are to regard producers as part of the 'intellectual elite', however, we must be clear about what precisely their area of expertise is. Garnham claims that, like priests, they are 'specialists in symbolic production and transmission' (2000: 83). This goes beyond Fischer's characterization of them being experts in a particular field of specialist knowledge, such as literature or science. Fischer recognized this, too, suggesting the BBC producer also needed 'good judgment of ideas and people'. Their professionalism is therefore something looser and more diffuse. The producer Lance Sieveking joined the BBC in the 1920s with no professional qualifications but having fought in the war, published poetry and novels, dabbled in journalism; he was also well connected in artistic, literary and political circles. His colleague, Lionel Fielden suggested that the core skill required was the ability to spot trends and ideas and, above all, the right sort of people to put on air – and that this meant a 'constant alertness':

> the reading (or at least skimming) of every new book, the seeing of every new play and film, the attendance at every party to which one was asked, the journeys around England, to points where one thing or another created interest – slums, unemployment, pageants, new factories, a murder trial, a scandal, anything and everything: but above all an ear constantly cocked, at parties, in buses or tubes, at exhibitions, in shops, in the street and on the farm, for the Promising Voice.
>
> (Fielden, 1960: 10)

This vividly fleshes out our earlier definition of the producer's role – that is, to turn 'the best minds' into 'ancient mariners' before a national audience. But it's also a more democratic vision, for what is striking in Fielden's account is the sheer variety and range of subject matter and humanity being hunted down and embraced.

We might say, then, that one definition of professionalism in public service broadcasting is the ability to move lightly across traditional scholarly and social boundaries – to be, as it were, a professional amateur. If the producer has a specialism, it's the rather intangible one of being able to roam widely with confidence and then to 'metabolize': to sense the undercurrents of change in the world; to digest them and meditate on their significance; and finally, to find a way of relating these discoveries and ideas back to the lay audience at home. This kind of work both proceeds *from* and contributes *to* what Stefan Collini (2006) calls the 'discourse of general ideas'.

Thus put, the producer's role is obviously culturally very significant. But another aspect of this professionalism is that one does something because it needs to be done, rather than for reasons of self-aggrandizement or personal self-publicity. In the BBC this translates into a long-standing belief that it is the producer's job to be self-effacing. Reith phrased the original requirement in typically moralistic terms: 'they who do the most work and carry the greatest weight usually make the least amount of noise in doing so'. 'The desire for notoriety and recognition', he added, 'sterilizes the seeds from which greatness might spring' (1924: 52). But a more enduring justification for self-effacement is the aesthetic one: simply put, it is that if a producer's job is to 'mediate', he or she needs to avoid getting 'in the way' of the programme's raw material. There are temptations to do otherwise, of course: as we saw in Chapter 3, many producers have wanted to turn radio or television into distinctive new art forms by making their presence felt as artistic innovators in their own right. But generally speaking, the producer's task is to shape the raw material of others without really being *seen* to shape that material – not so much a misleading act, as an *enabling* one, designed to make the viewing or listening process as natural-seeming as possible. This is the producer as 'midwife', and explains Scannell's reference to broadcasting's hidden labour: the word 'hidden' is absolutely paramount, for although producers must get paid for their efforts, they should expect no thanks. If their efforts go unnoticed – if they're taken for granted – they will have succeeded. The hidden nature of broadcasting, I would suggest, is one of the things that turn it into a service.

Yet, seeming so effortless, of course, means it is taken for granted. The broadcasters' habitual concealment of their own efforts makes it easy for them to be accused of lacking the breadth of vision or the independence required for the job. Sartre once famously distinguished between 'intellectuals' and 'technicians of practical knowledge' – an idea since reformulated, first by Edward Said when he distinguished between 'amateur' and 'professional' intellectuals, and more recently by Frank Furedi in his attack upon what he sees as a media taste for 'talking heads servicing the show' by supplying 'easily digestible portions of knowledge and culture' (Garnham, 2000: 87; Furedi, 2006: 23–4, 40). The critique, in essence, is that true public value comes from intellectuals rising above their narrow specialisms, and being able to challenge orthodoxies rather than produce them – a critical role too easily abandoned. Even more prevalent, however, is the argument that broadcasters should not set themselves up as privileged specialists in 'symbolic production and transmission' in the first place, since the intellectual work of media production is – and should increasingly be – democratized. With less and less room for an agreed 'canon' of great art or literature, or even for the idea of universal values, it is argued that there is less and less point in a division of labour that puts some people in charge of interpreting the world on our behalf. Indeed, institutions, *by their very nature*, have become suspect entities in modern life. There has long been a school of thought that sees the French Revolution of 1789 and its bloody aftermath as clear evidence that giving power to idealists driven by abstract notions is inherently dangerous. Similarly, the sociologist Max Weber has outlined the potentially oppressive character of a society run according to reason and logic in the pursuit of efficiency – the so-called rule of 'instrumental reason', in which we are freed by bureaucracy from dogma and favouritism but denied full imaginative or expressive freedom, and we therefore end up disenchanted, imprisoned in effect, by the controlling 'iron cage' of rationality. It's a rich theme, mined by many others since. The implication of all these approaches is that we should see those employed in large bureaucratic organizations such as the BBC as the complicit operatives of an ideological regime. For, as Michael Bailey reminds us, 'many radicals see the media as a de facto functionary of the state and the ruling political elite' (2010: 234).

A second major critique of public service professionalism is that its practitioners have simply drifted over time into inward-looking, uninspired patterns of behaviour. It's easy to see that bureaucracies by their nature can become a little sclerotic, perhaps a little disdainful of public feeling. Some of this was detected in the case of British broadcasting in the

1960s, by the sociologist Tom Burns, and again, in the 1990s, by the anthropologist Georgina Born. After observing the BBC at work for extended periods, both concluded that, in place of free-flowing debate, there were signs of a recalcitrant belief among staff that things are as they are simply because this was the way things were done – that in place of open debate there was habit reinforced by mutual defensiveness (Burns, 1977; Born, 2005). Burns focused, in particular, on BBC journalists, and thought there'd been a marked shift away from devotion to public service ideals towards an inward-looking professionalism in which they valued the autonomous appraisal of fellow journalists above all other judgements, either internally or externally. Three decades on, with the BBC under its Director-General John Birt going through a period of intense market-driven reorganization, Born noted a slightly different mind-set taking grip beneath the Corporation's defensive exterior: a diminishing appreciation of 'craftsmanship' or creativity based on experience, imbued values or instinct, and, in its place, an atmosphere of nervous populism, with producers made to conform to 'product templates dictated by centralised commissioning according to the ersatz accountability of market analysis and research' (Born, 2005: 372; Sennett, 2006: 98–127).

A third line of attack on BBC professionalism has come from the neo-liberal Right – increasingly nowadays in alliance with advocates of 'new' or 'do-it-yourself' social media. It is based on Hayek's idea that 'collectivism in the end cannot tolerate freedom of thought'. The ideology has been expressed in countless different ways over the years. In the 1950s, for example, the economist Ronald Coase criticized the BBC on the basis that any centralized body of broadcasters determining what was good and bad on behalf of the general public represented 'a totalitarian philosophy' (O'Malley, 2009: 28). More recently, the former Winchester College and Oxford-educated British Ambassador Peter Jay has (apparently without irony or self-awareness) dismissed BBC staff for believing themselves to be the 'betters' of their fellow citizens, arguing that in a democracy the whole goal of raising the cultural level of a society is an illegitimate enterprise, since it 'arrogates to self-appointed' individuals what should be everyone's free choice of cultural tastes (Jay, 2009: 78–81). What all these critiques share is the belief that a concentration of power – any concentration of power – is likely to be dangerous. But it is a belief also sometimes wrapped up with a more visceral loathing of the BBC's Enlightenment ethos. Thus, for example, the ability of producers in a station such as Radio 1 to 'mould' British popular music tastes by selecting which tracks go on their playlist is a kind of hegemony no less malignant because it's done in the name of public service rather than through market forces (see Frith, 1978;

Hendy, 2000). In the end, what unites all these criticisms is unease at the BBC producer's extraordinary cultural power to choose what goes on air, and so have a controlling influence on the shape of national culture or the boundaries of national political debate.

Faced with this confluence of scepticism, public service broadcasters have often deployed an obvious defensive strategy: stressing their inherent pluralism, while laying less and less stress on their mission to 'lead' and more and more on a willingness to 'follow'. The shift in attitudes was articulated forcefully by one of the BBC's senior news editors, who in 1969 declared in an internal memo that 'the idea of information and education by stealth, of do goodism to the untutored masses, is wholly, and rightly, dead ... . We are not here to influence but to serve' (BBC WAC, 1969). It is important to recognize that this particular editor wasn't calling for demanding programmes to be replaced by more popular ones; indeed, his point was precisely that the BBC should avoid diluting its journalism simply in order to 'reach out' to a broader audience. Nevertheless, his positioning of the two objectives – 'to influence' and 'to serve' – as mutually contradictory is a striking rejection of what's surely long been a key Reithian principle, namely that the BBC serves *by* influencing. As Reith himself wrote, 'We ourselves set the pace, and in doing so gave ourselves the task of keeping up with it, of developing in advance of suggestions from without' (1924: 27). In this formulation, BBC producers and editors serve the public by being a little ahead of public opinion and by being willing to shape it. This is why Reith saw staff as 'inventors' rather than 'mechanics', and one of his spiritual descendants at the BBC in the 1970s and 1980s, Ian McIntyre, talked of 'architects' rather than 'builders' (see Hendy, 2007). Whatever the precise description, it's clear, both from the 1969 memo on the one side, and these classical Reithian definitions – still heard, even if less forcefully – on the other, that there's no settled view of what exactly the 'professionalism' of a producer entails, other than a general concern for high standards, a commitment to broadcasting for the public rather than for personal gain and a general ethos of impartiality.

Essentially, though, the issue boils down to whether or not we still accept the notion of a traditional division of labour between 'intellectuals' and the rest of us. This division involves delegating to public service broadcasters the right to choose and select what we watch and hear. In a culture heavily shaped by the notion of consumer choice, the very idea of letting someone else decide on our behalf seems utterly illiberal, even unnecessary. It seems to proceed from a deeply old-fashioned assumption that the public are like children, in need of guidance –

which is, of course, precisely why Reithianism's so often described as an example of 'Paternalism'. Yet, if broadcasters are required to tread carefully around such matters, we might nevertheless still allot them the task of carrying into the public realm what Edward Said called 'the culture of critical reason'. After all, society at large still operates on the basis of clear divisions of labour. We are happy to let doctors diagnose our illnesses, trained teachers educate our children, and lawyers or judges protect our freedoms. It's entirely reasonable, therefore, to let broadcasters – that is, people whose particular skill lies in metabolizing the world and reflecting it back to us in new and interesting ways – to go about their business on our behalf. This notion surely applies all the more so if we regard television and radio as welcome forms of relaxation in the interstices of our own working days: we are, quite literally, paying the broadcasters to entertain and inform and educate us – to do the work for us so that we don't have to. Passivity has a bad press; but most of us rely on it – indeed, crave it – for some part of our daily lives. Furthermore, the specific notion of expertise still has traction. For, if producers in particular areas of programme-making are truly knowledgeable in their allotted subject matter, they are also more likely than the rest of us to be able to make informed judgements about what might entertain, inform or educate. Peter Jay has suggested that the BBC's chief failure is that its producers regard themselves as 'better' than the licence-fee payers. But this is to misread them. Most producers regard their task simply as ensuring that a richer range of human activity reaches the screen or loudspeaker *than would be the case if it were left either to market forces or to the force of aggregated public demand* – forces that intrinsically favour the familiar over the new. Creating completely new programmes proceeds, at some point, from a leap of faith – or, more precisely, a following of developed instinct – by broadcast staff. It remains a powerful argument in favour of allowing broadcasters their traditional freedom of action if we simply point out that hugely successful series such as *The Hitchhiker's Guide to the Galaxy* (BBC Radio 4, 1978) or *The Office* (BBC TV, 2001–3), emerged not from any public demand for a 'sci-fi comedy' exploring the subject of existence or a comedy set in a Slough office exploring the banal desire within us to be famous, but from the imaginative capacities of writers and producers employed by the BBC itself – and by commissioning editors prepared to take the risk that we just might like what they come up with.

Expertise can, in fact, be reconciled with broadcasting's desire to be 'open' and inclusive. The BBC's Director-General Hugh Greene articulated the general position when he said more than four decades ago that he wanted the microphone and the television screen to be 'available to the widest possible range of subjects and to the best exponents available of the differing views on any given subject' so that those with differing views might come 'to know and understand each other's attitudes' (Greene, 1969: 13–14, 94). As Greene, once argued, 'Broadcasting's true objectives' are 'not "conversions" but rather the "breaking down of barriers"' (BBC, 1965: 4). In other words, since Reith – and sometimes even during Reith's administration – the BBC's been more about exposing us to things – ideas, art, knowledge – that might otherwise pass us by in our day-to-day, busy, working lives. Which is why, one BBC figure suggested, the role of someone running a channel such as BBC Radio 4 is to act 'like a friend who has read a few more books, seen a bit more of the world' (Hendy, 2007: 3). This might appear a rather modest goal. But that, too, is precisely the point. Broadcasters are there to carry forward the intellectual's traditional Enlightenment goals – but in gentle, even surreptitious, ways.

The proper functioning of all these factors depends, ultimately, on us accepting another underlying principle: the inherent value of a 'bureaucratic' approach to public affairs. Bureaucracy, of course, has had as bad a press as passivity. Modern bureaucracies, with their 'consistent, methodically prepared and precisely executed relations of command and obedience' are, viewed in strictly Weberian terms, merely the sinister tools of our political regimes; they 'compel conformity' and are utterly impersonal, concerned only with the most efficient way of running affairs (Scannell, 2007: 40–2). But it's also worth noting that the very impersonality of bureaucracies might also, in some senses, be to their credit. They operate, as Weber said, 'without regard for particular persons and situations'. Thus, Scannell suggests:

> They do not take personal considerations into account in any aspect of their work. This impersonality is principled. It abolishes favouritism, nepotism and bribery – in short, what were regarded as corruption in older systems of administration which modern bureaucracies are designed to replace. Those who work in bureaucracies are not the personal servants or property of those who appoint them. Appointments are based on merit, not on personal considerations of friendship, kinship or gain. Even those who hold high office, do so on the same principle. The post is separable, in principle and practice, from the person who holds it. Anyone can be sacked for failing to meet the requirements of the post.

(42)

In the end, then, while acknowledging with Weber the tendency of bureaucracies to become mechanical and unfeeling, we also need to recognize that their very impersonality and 'detachment' – their aloofness, if you like – is the price to be paid if we want our broadcasters to be editorially and culturally impartial, for them to do as Matthew Arnold wrote, namely 'to rise above' the idea of class or sectional interests and create some sort of 'organ of our collective best self, of our national right reason' (1875: 83).

Conscience

What stops public service broadcasters from betraying the trust we place in them? The usual answer is 'conscience'. And it's by focusing on conscience that we might better understand how it is that public service broadcasters claim to be able, all at once, to follow their own intellectual instincts, take into account public feelings and yet remain somehow 'impersonal'. It's also how we might get to grips with one of the most misunderstood aspects of a big public organization like the BBC, namely the idea of it as a 'self-managing bureaucracy'.

The classic articulation of the 'conscience' of the producer came from Hugh Greene when he was Director-General. In a speech, he pointed out that, like Britain, the BBC had 'no written constitution': it was governed more by precedence and experience than by legal instruments' (BBC, 1965: 6). As a result, conventions had accumulated over the years, and these had 'almost' – but 'not quite' – the force of law (7). That difference between 'almost' and 'not quite' is vital. For through it Greene implies there's a kind of 'sixth sense' inculcated within each producer as to what's right and what's not. This is what allows the producer to pursue his or her intellectual goals responsibly – that is, without any outside interference or fiercely rigid code of conduct. The word 'responsibly' is, of course, problematic: it can easily imply a degree of timidity in the face of authority, perhaps a hint of self-censorship. For Greene, this was one reason why 'cultural arbiters', such as the clergy, MPs, newspaper columnists and grass-roots complainants, should always be denied direct control over the day-to-day work of broadcasters (8–9). Yet this protection was also emphatically not about giving producers 'total licence' (7–8). It has been reiterated for decades that one of the fundamental features of broadcasting is that it enters every home and can take people by surprise. So programme-makers need to be conscious, Greene said, of 'what it is proper to put forward to an audience which may run into millions' (9–10, 13).

So should broadcasters interpret their public duty to be that of find-ing – and working at – the median point between artistic licence and a more cautious register of public taste? Not quite, according to Greene. He argued that programmes must be made 'on the assumption that the audience is capable of reasonable behaviour and of the exercise of intel-ligence – and of choice' (9). The audience, in fact, should be thought of as 'a series of individual minds (each with its own claim to enlighten-ment, each of different capacity and interests) and not as that statistical abstraction the "mass" audience' (9–10). Given that the 'mass audience' was an abstraction of real people with a huge variety of interests and attitudes, 'no subject – no subject whatever – can be excluded from the range of broadcasting simply for being what it is ... relevance is the key' (9–10). However, when it came to treatment – *how* the subject should be tackled on air – Greene said this 'demands the most careful assessment of the reasonable limits of tolerance' (10). Thus, for example, by the end of the 1960s the BBC was tolerating, say, nudity on screen and 'strong' language on air – but only where producers felt sure it was 'artis-tically' justified (see Hendy, 2006). As the Director-General said, while outrage may be wrong, 'Provocation can be healthy and, indeed, socially imperative' (BBC, 1965: 10).

Greene – and his period in office, the 1960s – was, of course, a high-water mark of progressive attitudes across much of the Western world. But what he said then merely articulated more explicitly an attitude that, with some modification, survives in public service broadcasting to this day. The BBC's most recent editorial guidelines, for instance, state that 'care must be taken' not to cause offence over, say nudity or bad language. Their use is not banned; but they 'must be justified by the context' and 'subject to careful consideration'. Similarly, 'frank and real-istic portrayals of sex and the exploration of themes and issues' related to sex are also permitted: the formal guidelines make clear that the issue, again, is rather that the BBC 'must be able to justify' its treatment of these subjects (BBC, 2011).

All this 'careful consideration' is usually an internal process – part of that 'hidden labour'. And, as such, it is an example of a public service broadcaster acting as a 'self-managed bureaucracy'. In the BBC this amounts, in particular, to two important but frequently misunderstood processes: 'reference upwards' and 'retrospective review'. 'Reference upwards' relates to the requirement that individual programme-makers refer a matter to their editorial superiors for adjudication if it's particu-larly serious, sensitive or complex, and that such editors might then refer the matter to their seniors – and so on, right up to the Director-General if necessary. This is not quite a traditional chain of command. Such is the never-ending vastness of output that senior executives would be unable to cope if there were 'referrals' constantly coming their way. So, producers have to be trusted to identify for themselves an issue that needs reference upwards, 'guided', as the former BBC Director-General Charles Curran put it, 'only by the general philosophy of the organisation' and by their own 'recognition of that philosophy' (1979: 135). In live radio or television, there is often no time to 'refer upwards' anyway. Producers must therefore be capable of 'careful consideration' by instinct. Which is why, in Greene's words, judgements must spring 'from some ingrained code' (BBC, 1965: 13).

For a code to be 'ingrained' it has to be understood at a deep level. And this can come, in the BBC's case, from the cumulative impact of 'retrospective review'. Put at its most basic, this refers to the long-established practice by which finished programmes are only 'reviewed' by senior executives *after* they've been broadcast. This is not to say that there's no editorial oversight during a programme's pre-production. Rather, it refers to the BBC belief that once a programme has been commissioned, and a producer entrusted with its completion, he or she must be left as free of outside interference as possible. To do otherwise might damage their ability to take risks and realize their vision. If what they end up with in some sense 'fails' they will learn from their mistakes and perhaps succeed the next time: in this way, there is room for editorial skills to be built up through trial and error, and with the benefit of ongoing feedback. The concept of 'retrospective review' also relates to a much deeper BBC assumption – namely, that instead of demand dictating supply, supply might dictate demand. Take, for instance, this comment by Alasdair Milne, the BBC's Director-General in the 1980s:

> broadcasters do not produce programmes they think are good for the rest of us, as the most often repeated sneer against public service broadcasting implies. They make the programmes they are keenest to make and believe in. It is then the public which ultimately decides whether it is interested in a particular idea, treatment or strand. Thus, over the years, programmes which started with tiny audiences have become national talking points. That is how archaeology, natural history, science programmes – or snooker, which is the most dramatic example – gripped the attention of millions of people. Had they been asked *before* seeing any of these whether they were interested in Rameses the Second or the mating habits of frogs or black

holes, they might have, ever so politely, sent you packing ... . The decisive element of surprise and novelty essential to any public service network would be absent.

(Milne, 1988: 211–12)

In other words, being able to make a programme before gauging public or critical reaction is a key guarantor of surprise and novelty. This is why the BBC, historically, has had a more ambivalent attitude to audience research than the commercial sector: seeking to respond to audience 'wants' might be *part* of the BBC's remit, but it could never be the *whole* of its remit, since that would most likely bring a halt to the creativity of producers charged with the duty to take a leap into the unknown. Not a complete leap into the unknown, of course, since, places such as the BBC have a mechanism known as 'Programme Review' for inculcating a 'general philosophy'. At the BBC, this consists of a regular meeting at which senior producers, editors, heads of department and channel controllers 'review' programmes broadcast over the past week, and discuss the editorial, aesthetic and policy implications that arise. It is a kind of collective brain – a forum for the clash of debate, which, though confidential, helps a large broadcasting institution to evolve and reify its codes and values. Minutes are taken and then circulated to senior staff, so that policy filters down through the various layers of the organization. Standards are thus set by a rolling process of peer review – an ethos of constant self-questioning (Hendy, 2007: 91).

It's not hard to see why some outside observers might be critical of this process. There is no guarantee that the 'clash of debate' is really a free exchange of ideas, rather than a 'taking of sides' among various interest groups, nor that the broadcasting philosophy which emerges will be anything other than a bland, middling, compromise. Sometimes, too, there is the risk of a particular ideology taking hold. Since the 1980s, for example, large institutions like the BBC have increasingly fallen under the influence of a 'managerialist' ideology (Sennett, 2006; Hendy, 2007: 284–97). And in recent years, programme-makers have grumbled about a culture of 'compliance', in which guarantees about conforming to editorial standards are sought in advance of production. In these circumstances, it's easy to see why the number of detailed written guidelines for BBC staff has been growing. Such documents emerge from a loss of trust in public institutions – something often encouraged by advocates of private enterprise. The BBC, along with universities, schools, hospitals and local councils, now needs to be both accountable and *seen* to be accountable. As a result, all these public bodies are increasingly forced to quantify intrinsically *un*quantifiable values, such as 'quality' or 'creativity'.

Even so, certain principles endure, and there is a residual resistance to reducing the producer's role to that of a mere operative on an assembly line. The culture of continuous internal debate that arises, in order to avoid strict codes – what outside critics see as an inefficient and sometimes stifling tendency to discuss everything *ad nauseam* – does at least create the possibility of a nuanced response to social and cultural change in the world outside: flexibility is hard-wired into the system. This is important. The BBC is often accused of being a closed world, characterized by an inward-looking professionalism. But programme-makers don't measure themselves solely against the judgement of their peers. In a forum such as the Review Board they also discuss newspaper comments, debates in Parliament and letters, phone calls and emails from the public; indeed the BBC as a whole receives hundreds of thousands of such communications, and there's a system in place for ensuring the most important comments reach production departments. Hence programming decisions arise from a complex mosaic of considerations:

> the personal instincts of Controllers and producers, yes, but also a sense of how any given programme fitted the Corporation's ethos, a calculation of the political or critical climate, the pragmatic dictates of time and money, the constant weighing of public attitudes.
>
> (Hendy, 2007: 401)

In short, there is in public service broadcasting a delicate equilibrium – and deliberately so – between the private instincts of the producer, the overall culture and ethos of the organization and the temperature of public opinion outside: no single ingredient can dominate.

Creativity

Finally, what about creativity? Can it ever thrive in large public service institutions? It is usually understood as springing from the autonomous freedom of the individual to act according to his or her vision: in other words, it is an intrinsically individualist phenomenon, and, as such, appears to be fundamentally incompatible with the bureaucratic ethos of a large organization replete with systems, routines, collective habits and the inevitable administrative inertia that comes with time. Yet I wish, in this final section, to argue that large, bureaucratic public service broadcasters are not always inimical to experiment, and that it is precisely when 'traditional' public service approaches have been replaced by those from the commercial sector that broadcasters such as the BBC have done most damage to their own creative powers. Conversely, I would argue, it is when organizations such as the BBC have been 'true' to their so-called 'inefficiencies' that creativity has been most alive.

Take for instance the early 1990s, when the BBC's Director-General at the time, John Birt, introduced a new working regime with the rather Orwellian title of 'Producer Choice'. This entailed an 'internal market', supposedly designed to squeeze inefficiencies out of the system by making each individual programme team or department responsible not only for their direct costs but also for a share of the hitherto hidden overheads. The hope was that producers would, for instance, avoid using studios for longer than they really needed now that 'overruns' proved costly. The BBC was also split in half: those who commissioned programmes, such as the channel controllers, became 'purchasers'; those who came up with the programmes, or provided certain support services, became 'providers'. The latter – now grouped into so-called 'business units' – would try to sell their 'goods' to the former. Birt's assumption was that competition would thereby drive down costs and rid the BBC of 'excess capacity'. It is hard to conclude anything but that the effect of all this on creativity was negative: producers were spending more time on budgets and paperwork at the expense of thinking about the programmes they were actually making; there were financial incentives to reduce the time spent on ensuring high production values, and penalties in place for working by instinct rather than preconceived format; meanwhile, the whole ethos of working in a team – or as part of 'One BBC' – was displaced by an expanding network of relationships based on trade and competition. Observing the experience of the Television Drama group, in particular, Georgina Born concluded that there'd been real 'erosion' in its creative autonomy and confidence (2005: 304).

As Richard Sennett points out, when people are required to act like consumers, they cease to think like 'craftsmen'. Craftsmanship – the pursuit of quality for its own sake through an ongoing process of trial and error – is rarely enhanced by the intrusion of market pressures. So public service broadcasting, though always for the public, appears to function most creatively when it's insulated to some extent from it – and from the commercial world. Competition induces a kind of nervous populism – clumsy attempts to 'lighten' programme content, to make output more 'accessible' (Hendy, 2007). In steering clear of giving the public something they haven't asked for, broadcasters also deny themselves the chance to break away from convention and surprise the public – to create something truly *new*. Indeed, there is evidence that, creatively speaking, tolerating a certain amount of chaos and inefficiency is highly productive: it is what allows for the trial and error involved in forging successful formats from experimental ones. On BBC Radio 1, for example, this tolerance can be detected in the career of John Peel, whose eclectic and sometimes 'difficult' choice of music was allowed on air on the most popular mainstream pop station in Britain almost continuously between 1967 and his premature death in 2004. He was the antithesis of highly formatted – and thus highly predictable – music radio. And in marketing or audience-research terms, he made no sense whatsoever, since his very eclecticism made him uncategorizable. Radio 1's tolerance of his individuality would have been virtually unthinkable within the commercial sector. As it was, Peel's shows became outstanding examples of what Paul Long calls the 'discourse of amateurism' – not so much a reference to his habitual mis-cueing of vinyl discs, but to a kind of *anti*-professionalism, an engagement with music for itself, rather than for gain (2006: 43). In fact, Peel perfectly embodies the BBC's willingness to see the long-term benefits to public culture of *un*predictability.

Creativity goes beyond the tolerant accommodation of individual talents. It is also about the possibilities offered by working within a large institution – even a large bureaucratic institution. Size itself can be a virtue, creating critical mass. The Drama department in BBC Radio is, for example, the largest single commissioner of drama in the world; the Light Entertainment department the largest commissioner of comedy; the BBC as a whole the largest broadcast newsgathering operation in the world. These activities do not just ensure a ready supply of breadth and depth in BBC output; they feed British culture as a whole – providing a training ground, a place to test new ideas and new talent away from the commercial pressures that demand generic conventions and instant success. The fact that a range of very different activities exists in close adjacency is also helpful: a process of cross-fertilization becomes possible – a creative clash of cultures as producers from different departments talk together in the same corridors and canteens. Indeed, even the reality of working in an organization replete with established procedures and guidelines might be as much of a stimulus as a constraint. Or rather, it might be a stimulus because it's a constraint. In his pioneering work on painting, Ernst Gombrich (1960) suggested that, for artists, at least, some boundaries and rules are necessary simply because they can only push through to something new by appreciating what they are pushing *against*. Where *everything* is possible and *nothing* expected the creative process often grinds to a halt: variety only comes when 'schema' are in place to begin with.

One thing that almost certainly needs to be in place is a clear motive for broadcasting in the first place. It's been suggested that there are three vital pre-conditions for creativity to thrive in any organization: critical thinking skills, expertise and motivation (Amabile, 1998). Of these, motivation – a sense of purpose – is apparently the most important. And the best kind of motivation is intrinsic. When discussing motivation, Richard Sennett refers to the importance of workers 'feeling useful' – and that very often this means having a sense of 'contributing something which matters to other people' (2006: 187–9). He notes, too, that doing this for a public institution tends to heighten this feeling that the work matters (190–3). We might conclude, therefore, that a shared and easily graspable sense of corporate purpose – a sense, say, that one's programmes make a difference to people's lives – is, in itself, a spur for creativity. The American writer David Foster Wallace put much the same point rather eloquently, when he suggested that 'the big distinction between good art and so-so art lies somewhere in the art's heart's purpose, the agenda of consciousness behind the text. It's got something to do with love' (Smith, 2009: 259).

Love might seem too grand and romantic a word to end with in a chapter having the mundane title 'service'. But it captures that sense of devotion to the work itself that has always supposedly been a feature of employment at public service broadcasters such as the BBC. It also speaks to the way the whole process involves thoughtfulness towards *others*. Indeed, the relationship between broadcasters and their audiences is at the heart of it all. The broadcasters don't really produce programmes they think are good for us, Alasdair Milne explained: they usually 'make programmes they are keenest to make and believe in', and it is then the public which decides whether it is interested in what is on offer (1988: 211). This is why a BBC figure such as George Fischer conceives of his and his fellow broadcasters' position as having been '*licensed* by the public and by Parliament to exercise our judgement' (interview, 2003). There is a process of delegated responsibility here, a division of labour. *They* produce; *we* audit. Admittedly, the tensions remain. There's still an implicit view in many criticisms of public service broadcasting that producers are intellectual outsiders, 'always in danger of failing fully to appreciate or understand the rich diversity' of everyday, normal, popular culture (Garnham, 2000: 128). In one sense this is true, for ultimately their role rests on a paradox: to be most effective in the public service, they need to some extent to insulate themselves from the public. We license the freedom this bestows in the hope and expectation that we will be repaid in the longer run – by workers using television and radio to fashion 'a "we" language that speaks to common values, common problems, a common heritage, a common sense of the historical moment ... shared across the boundaries that divide intellect from public life' (Rosen, 1994: 369). To defend the concept of the public sphere is to defend a protected realm: an unfashionable position. But in making this deal – in granting broadcasters a sense of agency – we also end up serving ourselves.

5 Choice: Responding to Competition

As the final decade of the twentieth century began, it was agreed that 'an epoch in the history of broadcasting' was 'coming to a close' (Scannell and Cardiff, 1991: 3). Although there had been a commercial system in America and state-run services in many other countries, until the 1980s radio and television across much of the developed world had been dominated by big national public service corporations – the BBC in Britain, NRK, Sveriges Radio and YLE in Scandinavia, the CBC in Canada, the ABC in Australia and so on. They'd not just stood in powerful opposition to commercial broadcasting; they'd 'dominated the cultural geology of the societies from which they had been formed' (Tracey, 1998: 40). From the 1970s onwards, however, this dominance had been challenged almost everywhere, as state regulation or national monopolies were cut back, new commercial competitors entered the arena and the number of available channels multiplied exponentially.

The rise of a market-dominated approach to broadcasting and its effect on the overall organization of the structures of radio and television is a story that has already been told elsewhere (see Crisell, 2002; O'Malley, 1994; Douglas, 1999; Mosco, 1996; Østergaard, 1997; Hendy, 2000a). In this chapter, therefore, I want to focus on two much more specific questions: how these changes have been justified on the basis of public service broadcasting's alleged inability to offer real choice to listeners and viewers, and how public broadcasters might be able to challenge these allegations – and perhaps redefine the terms of a debate too often dominated by a reductive ideology of choice. My argument is not that a wide choice in what goes on air is necessarily bad. It is that public service broadcasting – even in its more monopolistic forms – might actually be a better provider of choice than the commercial system. Moreover, I want to suggest that public service broadcasting, because it sets out to make us better informed at making choices, provides a vital underpinning for that 'marketplace' of ideas and cultural products which characterizes our contemporary broadcasting ecology.

The 'Logic' of Choice

It is choice, as a concept, which lies behind many of the debates about competition. This is because choice is invariably associated with the freely expressed will of an autonomous individual. And while a marketized system appears to be an inherently individualistic enterprise, concerned with allowing each of us to express a preference and have that preference satisfied, public service broadcasting has long appeared to be an inherently collective enterprise concerned with that aggregate entity 'the public' – and with imposing its own values upon that public. There's some truth to this distinction. As we've seen in previous chapters, an institution such as the BBC has long assumed that radio and television should provide what people need rather than what they want – an approach which has appeared to be not just insensitive to public demand, but, for much of its history, deliberately so. Moreover, even though the BBC and its foreign counterparts have long since tried to embrace public taste, they've been accused of being too large, too bureaucratic, too close to the state or the establishment, too middle class or too liberal-minded, to do so effectively. As the Annan Committee put it, when assessing the health of the British system in the mid-1970s, the original Arnoldian–Reithian model looked increasingly incapable of accommodating 'the variety of expression of what is good' (Curran and Seaton, 1997: 324). Indeed, public service broadcasting has consistently been compared unfavourably with 'the real choice' offered to consumers by a deregulated market (313, 344).

In the 1980s, this unfavourable comparison was made as part of a wider ideological challenge nurtured by the Right – which asserted that 'social good flows not from collective activity organized from the top down, but from a myriad individual decisions organized from the bottom up, rooted in the right of the individual to choose' (Tracey, 1998: 17). Consumers, from this standpoint, are deemed to be the best judges of what is in their own interests – and broadcasters, by implication, are required to relinquish their historic role as cultural arbiters. Thus, the head of the US Federal Communications Commission, argued in 1981 that henceforth 'the public's interests must determine the public interest' (48). In Britain, a few years later, the Peacock Committee, appointed by Margaret Thatcher's government, asserted that 'consumer sovereignty' should similarly hold sway: viewers and listeners, it said, would best satisfy their own interests 'if they have the option of purchasing the broadcasting service they require from as many alternative sources of supply as possible' (48). Technical innovation furnished the opportunity:

cable, satellite, digital multiplexes and pay-per-view or subscription technology all promised virtually unlimited capacity for programme services as well as a perfect matching up of supply and demand – destroying old arguments for rationing output because of spectrum scarcity. In short, market liberalization – working hand in glove with new technology – was all about liberating expressions of individual choice which had long been frustrated by public service broadcasting elites foisting their narrow tastes on everyone else.

The challenge this presented can hardly be exaggerated. If the programme output of public service broadcasters is to be conceived purely as a private commodity – that is, something valued only for its ability to satisfy individual desires – then the inherent ideology of broadcasting as a 'public good', let alone the core belief that broadcasting is capable of enhancing the quality of culture or democratic debate within a public sphere, crumbles to dust. An organization such as the BBC becomes simply one more supplier of radio and television programmes among others, undeserving of special status or privileged funding.

How on earth does public service broadcasting respond? Clearly, it could simply engage wholeheartedly in the battle for audiences within the marketplace. But in this case, if a public service broadcaster's programmes don't get watched or listened to, the market enthusiasts would quickly say that its creative inadequacy is exposed for all to see, while if its programmes do get decent ratings, the market enthusiasts would quickly say that it was obviously delivering the same consumer products as its commercial rivals, and thus its claim for special status and funding was illegitimate. And indeed, competing aggressively for ratings and competitive scheduling almost certainly leads to the slow attrition of core commitments to, for instance, quality drama or investigative journalism. As Georgina Born put it succinctly, a broadcaster like the BBC is 'damned if it does and damned if it doesn't' when it comes to trying to meet consumer demands (2005: 54–5). At best, it faces the accusation that it lacks 'focus': as one acute observer put it, it might soon be 'dead for lack of definition' (Steemers, 2001: 70).

In practice, then, publicly funded broadcasters have limited freedom of action. Unless, that is, they challenge the whole notion that commercial operators within a deregulated, 'fragmented' media ecology really do provide a greater choice than regulated, unitary public service broadcasters such as themselves – and assert instead that it is public service broadcasting, not the commercial sector, that wins in the competition to offer meaningful choice.

Improving Choice

If public service broadcasters wish to claim that it is they that offer greater choice, they will have to reject vigorously any notion that their role is to provide merely an 'essential' service in the face of occasional market failures. This, indeed, is how Peacock saw the future role of the BBC: as broadcasting opera, or book readings, or foreign news or other such things that the market might neglect to supply through a perceived lack of sufficient demand (Scannell, 2000: 55). It is how today's leading advocates of a marketized system, such as the Conservative Party advisor David Elstein, also see the BBC's role: a severely reduced one, in which the Corporation is only a supplier of last resort, producing the sort of highbrow quality programmes that might be paid for by subscriptions. It's a conception that doesn't explain how 'quality' programmes might be funded on such a reduced subscription-only income model. It's also a hopelessly ahistorical position, in that it assumes wrongly that this has been the BBC's role since its birth – that its move into popular programming is a recent aberration. Moreover, it assumes that the market is remarkably efficient in delivering the broad range of programmes demanded by most people. And perhaps worst of all, it assumes there's no reason to even try to make available to the broader public all those programmes of 'minority' appeal now confined to a subscription-based ghetto. It represents not so much a 'trimming back' of the BBC as a wholesale inversion of its purpose as a national broadcaster seeking to make all its programmes universally accessible.

This nevertheless represents, in more radical neo-liberal form, the current position of public service broadcasting in America. National Public Radio and Public Broadcasting Service (PBS) television remain 'free-to-air' rather than subscription-based services, of course. But quite apart from having to exist on tiny levels of income, compared with their European counterparts – and thus have their output regularly interspersed with funding appeals or plugs for sponsors – NPR and PBS were always conceived, right from the start, as a limited response to market failure. Their function is precisely that envisaged by neo-liberal voices: to enter the market as programme suppliers of last resort, filling in the gaps left by a pre-existing commercial system that's been doing just fine in making programmes that most people want most of the time but doesn't see much advertising return in doing the minority stuff. It's proved almost impossible for the public broadcasters to transcend this pre-allotted, and highly marginal, role. There is some innovative, challenging and entertaining programming on many public radio and TV stations. But it rarely impacts upon a national consciousness. Writing in 2002, for example, Jack Mitchell described American public radio, then some thirty-five years' old, as 'serving narrow niche markets too small to interest commercial broadcasters' (2002: 406). He was trying to argue that this experience of serving niche audiences with high-quality public affairs programming gave it a distinctive selling point. But his argument rested, too, on an acceptance that public broadcasters had stopped 'pretending' that they could educate a whole nation or even a community, and had accepted that they were a mere supplement to an entertainment-centred mainstream (407).

From the BBC's perspective, this appears an utterly defeatist position, made worse by data which show the audience for American public broadcasting is largely confined to the 'well-educated, societally conscious' (416). It's a model in which people get precisely what they want, of course. But it leaves little room for them to experience discomforting argument or surprise. And it strips public radio of any power – or indeed, any inclination – to reach beyond its 'natural' constituency. The BBC, by way of contrast, is always acutely conscious of its popular support. One reason for this is based on the link between universal funding and universal reach. The licence fee could only be justified if the BBC continued to be watched or listened to by most households at some point in the week. If it were to be converted into a voluntary subscription, with some households opting out, the fee would inevitably rise; more subscribers would then cancel, and a downward spiral of decline would begin. Indeed, even a report commissioned by a Conservative government concluded that there was 'no level of subscription fee that would match the BBC's funding under the current system' (Curran and Seaton, 1997: 337). But another reason for the BBC's concern with reaching a broad mainstream audience concerns its intrinsically democratic credentials. In 1972 an internal BBC document identified two good reasons for continuing to broadcast popular television comedies. First, because they helped make watching the BBC attractive to a great number of people – and thus enhanced the chances of these viewers also being exposed to the Corporation's 'more serious programmes'; and second, because 'the absence of a light entertainment element ... could also have an impoverishing effect on the serious programmes' by making it harder for such programmes to relate to how 'large numbers of people are feeling, thinking, and talking' (BBC WAC, 1972). The argument, then, was essentially, about the need to remain 'in touch' with all its licence-fee payers, not just the vocal and powerful minority. Similar reasoning was used in 1994 by the former Director of the BBC's World Service, John Tusa, when he argued that requiring the BBC to focus on supplying highbrow programmes would betray its fundamental purposes. Rather than securing a niche for its future, he said, it would lead to its exile to 'a so-called high ground ... inhabited only by the sound of cow-bells' (Tusa, 1994: 10).

There is another fundamental reason for public broadcasting to resist pressure from commercial lobbyists and the political Right to shrink itself back to a high-ground niche: because the assumption that the market has successfully delivered choice in the mainstream arena is itself highly questionable. The commercial system's failures have been described eloquently by the American media theorist Todd Gitlin (2000). Most television, he says, is both 'ever changing and ever the same' – 'its variants are variations on known themes and formulas' (vii–viii). Innovations and differences between one 'product' and another are often entirely superficial. This is not because of some dastardly plot to lull us into uncritical, passive recipients of a given ideological message. It's the indirect result of networks 'trying to read popular sentiment and tailoring their schedules towards what they think the cardboard people they've conjured up want to see and hear':

> If they concoct a hit, for whatever reasons, competitive bet-covering dictates that it be imitated *ad nauseam*, creating the sense of a rampant trend ... . The trick is not only to read the restless public mood, but somehow to anticipate it and figure out how to encapsulate it in a show.
>
> (203–4)

Gitlin goes on to point out that the broadcasters' self-vaunted instincts are not extraordinary – they are merely 'schooled': programme executives claim to be flexible, but their flexibility is 'bounded by the conventional wisdom that circulates through their favoured media' (204–5). The consequences of this were articulated to devastating effect in 1961, when the newly appointed head of America's FCC, Newton Minow, described the primetime output of his country's commercialized TV system as a 'Vast Wasteland'. Sit down in front of the screen, he said, and

> You will see a procession of game shows, formula comedies about totally unbelievable families, blood and thunder, western good men, private eyes, gangsters, more violence, and cartoons, and endless

commercials, many screaming, cajoling, and offending – and most of all, boredom.

(Minow, 1961)

Even in Britain, where commercial television had been operating under a much tighter public service-orientated regulatory regime, the Pilkington Committee declared in 1962 that there was 'a lack of variety and originality, an adherence to what is safe, and an unwillingness to try challenging, demanding, and still more, uncomfortable subject-matter' (Scannell, 2000: 7).

It might be argued that the push towards liberalizing the broadcasting sector in the 1980s was designed precisely to shake up this state of affairs – bringing more choice by dramatically increasing the number of providers and channels on offer. But even the diversification of output since then has often been more apparent than real. Crisell (2002), for instance, points out that very often the proliferation of channels has tended to proceed well in advance of our capacity to produce enough original content to fill them. One result has been an increasing tendency for television to offer endless repeats of its most successful programmes and for the same programmes to appear on several channels over the course of the same week. The need for all commercial operators to turn a profit – and thus, inevitably, to try to both minimize costs and maximize audience ratings – is perhaps at the root of the problem. Indeed, it is the pressure on costs that creates an impoverished production base in the first place. Certain programme genres are, of course, intrinsically expensive – original full-cast drama and foreign news coverage being two obvious examples. And it's the pressure on ratings that creates an aversion to taking too many risks with unfamiliar or challenging programmes.

The empirical evidence here is quite unambiguous. Take drama. Whereas in 1969–70 ITV screened 112 single plays, ten years later it screened only thirteen – a dramatic decline (Crisell, 2002: 200). In this same period the BBC fought what Crisell describes as 'a stronger rear-guard action', featuring works by playwrights such as Alan Bennett, Trevor Griffiths, John Mortimer, Peter Nichols and William Trevor. This reflected a public service commitment, Crisell suggests, because it showed support for a form which 'made intellectual demands on the audience and created aesthetic satisfactions that could not be derived from the series or serial'; to abandon it would also have been 'to deny the television audience access to all the major dramatists of the past' (200). In radio the contrasts are even more striking. Though pre-television era

American commercial radio produced a great deal of high-quality drama, by the 1960s it was almost entirely gone: once networks had decided that radio had become a 'secondary' medium of background listening – ideal for music and news – there was no reason to expect from audiences the sustained attentive listening required by drama. In Britain, too, a small but promising drama base all but disappeared from the commercial sector once the regulatory regime was loosened. Yet the BBC has persisted in retaining a core staff of some thirty or so drama producers, in commissioning several hundred new plays each year and in broadcasting an afternoon play on most days of the week on its main speech channel, Radio 4. Indeed, BBC Radio still claims, with some justification, to be the largest single commissioner of new dramatic writing in the world (Hendy, 2007: 183–5).

A similar pattern of cost-cutting and risk aversion in the commercial sector – leading, ultimately, to a narrowed range of output – is also apparent in factual programming. In Britain, the combined expenditure of the commercial channels ITV, Channel 4 and Five on original children's programmes in 2008 was £11 million; across all other commercial channels in the UK it was about £10 million; at the BBC, however, it was £77 million (Barnett and Seaton, 2010: 330). Since regulatory requirements were relaxed in the 1980s and early 1990s, the commercial sector has, in effect, all but abandoned the notion of providing original television programmes for the country's 'citizens-in-waiting'. Meanwhile, a 2005 study of international coverage on British screens – a category including war reporting, history, wildlife, science – showed that, while the overall amount had increased significantly since 2003, this rise had 'been driven primarily by the BBC', and that Channel 4, since being 'freed' of its public service commitments, had 'consistently reduced' its own output (Seymour and Barnett, 2006: 1). As the study concludes, by default it is the public service broadcaster that is left playing 'a pivotal role in keeping British citizens informed and aware of other countries and other cultures' (36).

Market forces pursue their own logic: true diversity and choice is only made available if it makes financial sense to make it available. In reality, as Jean Seaton puts it, 'the high costs of entry, media concentration, advertising distortion, and commodification impose a largely invisible but potent form of censorship' (Curran and Seaton, 1997: 345). Commercial broadcasters, though, have to create the illusion of diversity. So we often witness a version of what Theodor Adorno called 'pseudo-individualization' and what Freudians would describe as the 'narcissism of small differences': where each 'new' format is projected as being unique, despite being very similar to its rivals in all its basic features. Surveying the American radio scene in 1999, for example, Susan Douglas noticed that, although there were about fifty officially listed formats, it was virtually impossible to detect any difference between, say, 'soft rock' and 'soft adult contemporary', or between 'hot country' and 'young country' (1999: 348). Hence, in radio as in television, the publicly described 'format' of each channel is 'more of a tool for branding' on crowded airwaves 'and for packaging audiences in a comprehensible way to advertisers than a guide to actual content' (Hendy, 2000a: 35–6).

There is, then, a strong basis for arguing that 'choice' isn't actually being delivered very successfully by a 'deregulated' commercial sector, whether in the UK or US or elsewhere. And it's on precisely this basis that an operator such as the BBC can start to build a case for it being public service broadcasting which vouchsafes, on balance, a more robust guarantee of diversity. One way in which it does so is simply by ensuring that certain kinds of programming which might not survive for long in a nervous, timid marketplace are 'protected', so that, whatever short-term vicissitudes in consumer taste occur, they might at least stand a chance of reaching a wide audience at some point or another. Radio drama and radio comedy, television foreign news, science documentaries, choral music and children's programmes – some of the genres regularly found on BBC Radio 4 or BBC1 TV – probably all fall into this category. They would all probably be classified rather misleadingly as belonging to that rather bland and monolithic-sounding format, 'speech'. But in reality, it is a remarkably eclectic offering. Indeed, for a broadcaster such as the BBC, what's being offered is a kind of 'diversity-within-unity'. There is the diversity achieved through supplying a coherent 'family' of channels or services – each one rather specific in range and style, appealing say to a particular age group or to a particular section of music fans – and then trying to ensure that listeners and viewers are nudged into moving between these generic or 'narrowcast' channels through regular cross-trailing. There is also the diversity achieved within a given 'specialist' channel. For instance, BBC3 is broadly designed to appeal to 'younger' viewers, and has plenty of light-weight 'reality' and entertainment series accordingly. But in the course of a season, it has also recently woven into its schedules programmes such as these: a fly-on-the-wall documentary series about young soldiers in Afghanistan, another series about young people facing major transplant operations and *The Boarding School Bomber* (2011), a well-received drama-documentary about the early life of a would-be terrorist. Then,

finally, diversity is found within each individual programme. For example, if we sample just one week at random of the BBC late-night current
affairs programme, *Newsnight*, in 2011 we find extended reports on,
among other things, allegations of phone-hacking by newspapers, the
use of cognitive-enhancing drugs, changes in 'green energy' policies,
girl gangs, how immigration restrictions affect workplaces, the role of
football in Dagestan, an interview with Umberto Eco about the
disgraced Right-wing Italian Prime Minister Silvio Berlusconi, allegations of torture and brutality by military forces in Egypt and the damage
caused in the Congo by city speculators running 'vulture funds'.

There comes a point, of course, when 'diversity' can be seen simply
as a lack of focus or direction. The carping refrain of the BBC's critics is
that it tries to do too much – aiming to please everyone a bit rather than
some people a lot. It's accused of being never quite competitive enough
– or never quite devoted enough to a 'core' mission of focusing on quality or minority-interest genres. But as Georgina Born points out, this
diversity-within-unity is all part of the BBC's 'purposefully mixed
cultural economy' (2005: 54–5). It's no accident that it continues to
provide a large element of 'mixed' programming on services such as
BBC1, BBC2 and Radio 4. This mix is itself reflective of its underlying
belief in the concept of 'the public', over and above the concept of individual consumers wishing to exercise their free will. In the strictest
sense, of course, none of it represents more choice for viewers or listeners. It still represents what the broadcasters themselves decide should be
available to us at any given time. But since we can only choose from
what is available, it's important to be clear about the extent to which it
is public service broadcasting which has widened the ideological and
aesthetic spectrum of goods and services over the years. Its record is at
least as impressive – and probably more so – than that of the deregulated commercial sector.

Transcending the Ideology of Choice

The discussion so far has proceeded largely on the basis that choice is in
itself an intrinsically good thing – and that the issue is simply whether
or not it's been delivered successfully, or deciding which system,
commercial or public service, is better at achieving this. But we should
perhaps close this chapter by exploring a number of arguments that
challenge this whole underlying assumption about choice in the first
place. Our notion of consumer sovereignty rests on the idea that *we* are

'the best judges' of what we ourselves want or need. Yet, unfashionable and undemocratic though it might appear to be, there are good reasons to doubt our own abilities – and whether, even if we have them, we wish to continually exercise them.

For instance, Renate Salecl, in her book *The Tyranny of Choice* (2011), argues that a culture that places so much emphasis on choice also 'burdens' the individual (13). The problem, she suggests, is that 'we are not only required to choose between products: we are asked to see our whole lives as one big composite of decisions and choices' (1). There is a process of constant decision-making, and this not only takes time and effort; it also creates a never-ending flow of disappointment. This is because the sense that something 'better' is always available somewhere 'leads us not to more satisfaction but rather to greater anxiety, and greater feelings of inadequacy' (3). Salecl also challenges 'rational choice theory' from the perspective of a trained psychologist. Its fatal weakness, she points out, is that it presupposes we always think before we act, and that we'll always seek to maximize the benefits and minimize the costs. In reality, our decisions depend on many external factors – especially the availability of reliable information on which to base our choice. In other words, our decisions are never really entirely our own anyway – and can be easily swayed by misinformation. But perhaps the most important point of all in Salecl's argument is that there's a social and political penalty to be paid for adopting this ideology of choice: when we start assuming that all our problems can be tackled by changing ourselves, social critiques are displaced by self-critiques. 'By working so hard at self-improvement', she writes, 'we lose the energy and ability to participate in any form of social change' (11).

If Salecl's conclusions appear exceptionally pessimistic, it's worth pointing out that she's hardly alone in raising such doubts about rational choice theory. Daniel Kahneman – a Nobel Laureate in Economics no less – also suggests we rethink our views on choice on the basis of new work in the psychology of decision-making (2011). When we make choices, he argues, we often do so quickly, intuitively, emotionally. Often this 'fast thinking' is useful – it works. But we also sometimes think more slowly, more deliberatively, more logically. And this second way of making choices is also useful. Indeed, probably more useful, because those quick, intuitive choices often let us down through their inherent biases. One such bias is the 'halo effect', which Kahneman illustrates thus: 'When the handsome and confident speaker bounds onto the stage ... you can anticipate that the audience will judge his comments more favourably than he deserves' (4). Given what we know about the persuasive powers of voice and appearance in shaping, say, television viewers' voting intentions, it's not hard to translate this idea of the 'halo effect' into the ability of mass media to sometimes seduce us into making the wrong choices about what programmes to watch or which version of events is most convincing.

There are, I think, two important implications here for broadcasting. The first proceeds from the uncanny echo of John Reith we can detect at this point: that notion that, until people have experienced something, 'few know what they want, and very few what they need' (1924: 34). It's on this basis that we can still make out a case for a continuing division of labour in the matter of decision-making, in which we delegate to others some responsibility for making broadcasting choices on our behalf. Salecl herself gives the example of medicine. Data show, for instance, that whereas people in general – including those who aren't ill – usually want to be offered a choice between different kinds of treatment, those who are genuinely and seriously ill reject the idea of choice and assert a strong preference to get just 'the best' treatment based on the 'best' advice as quickly as possible (2011: 55). In short, just below the surface there's a residual trust in the value of expertise – perhaps even a psychological need to hand over some responsibility for our decisions. Now, admittedly the question of which TV or radio programme to 'consume' hardly presents us with such life-and-death issues. But the same principle surely holds: if we accept that broadcasters are 'experts' in selecting programme material judiciously, based on years of experience behind the scenes, then it also seems reasonable to hand over to them some of the burdensome work of choosing output for us – a burden which the ethos of consumer sovereignty places on our own weary shoulders. This, anyway, was what seemed to be the case in Norway. One recent study of television use there found that, even though interactivity and choice was abundantly on offer in many homes, the vast majority of viewers chose to simply switch on and watch whatever appeared: at the end of the day they were simply too tired to face the additional 'work' of yet more decision-making (Gentikow, 2010).

So can we trust the broadcasters to choose well on our behalf? It's interesting to note what Kahneman says here. Organizations, he says, are generally better than individuals when it comes to avoiding errors: 'they naturally think more slowly and have the power to impose orderly procedures' (2011: 417–18). The 'wisdom of crowds', though usually applied to the general population, clearly works in amplified fashion when applied to a large but defined group of specialists. Naturally, these specialists, just like us, choose intuitively a lot of the time. Their intuitive choices, however, tend to be more accurate than ours. This is most easily explained by what Kahneman calls 'the effects of long practice' (11). In other words, he suggests that skill – something nurtured over time – is a significant factor in making good choices.

If this all sounds a little too passive, then it's important to point out that we, as viewers and listeners, are not to be left permanently power-less in this analysis. It is just that if we, too, want to make good choices, we need to become a little more like these experts: we need to nurture – or have nurtured – our own skills. 'What can be done about biases?' Kahneman asks. 'How can we improve judgments and decisions, both our own and those of the institutions that we serve and that serve us? The short answer is that little can be achieved without a considerable investment in effort' (417). In practice, this means we must keep taking into account the long-term public good of any given phenomenon and not just the immediate private benefits it might bring to a given indi-vidual. For consumers, as consumers, will naturally have no concern with, say, longer-term national priorities: they enact a kind of 'individ-ualist subjectivism' where universities, for example, become account-able to the students they 'serve' and broadcasters, similarly, to the listeners or viewers they 'serve'. But universities might also be seen as being accountable to society – and so, of course, could public service broadcasters. The common public purpose includes, among other things, what a much older government policy on universities called 'a common pursuit of knowledge and understanding', where everyone was 'initiated into a realm of free inquiry' – and thus serving 'the intel-lectual needs of the nation' (Collini, 2011). In short, the real need is for universities to nurture critical minds – and the more critical and alert people there are around, the better democratic society is served. In fact, it's all a question of who exactly is being served: the 'public' as merely an aggregate of individuals with individual wants and needs – or the public as a collective entity that's more than the sum of its parts? There's no doubt that public service broadcasting, by its very nature – like universities once upon a time – assumes that it is the latter that is at the heart of their mission as much as the former. It 'stresses the merits of social cohesion and mutual obligation in contrast to a neo-liberal perspective of contracting and exchanging individuals' (Curran and Seaton, 1997: 336). It tries to offset the growing atomization of society through inviting us 'to be part of a conversation about our condition' (Barnett and Seaton, 2010).

Which brings us to the question of struggle – that effort involved in learning which Daniel Kahneman mentioned earlier. Of the new regime for universities, Collini said the point at issue isn't so much that the student's viewpoint is irrelevant; it's that 'the model of the student as consumer is inimical to the purposes of education'. 'The paradox of real learning', Collini reminds us, 'is that you don't get what you "want" – and you certainly can't buy it. The really vital aspects of the experience of studying something ... are bafflement and effort ... a demanding and not always enjoyable process' (2011). Transferring Collini's critique to the realm of television and radio might appear reckless – especially when public service broadcasters have for so long been accused of offering too many 'worthy but dull' programmes in the interest of improving us (Jacka, 2003: 186). But there's a reasonable case to be made that public service broadcasters are in a good position to furnish just the right 'space' for this educative struggle – provided, that is, they carry on making programmes that are just a little more demanding than we might ask for, but not so demanding that they destroy their own chances of reaching a reasonable spread of viewers or listeners. Indeed, it's precisely through its ability to combine 'an ability to entertain with a grand ambition to inform, educate, stimulate and enrich' that we can say an organization such as the BBC treats its public 'as citizens rather than consumers' (Barnett and Seaton, 2010).

Naturally, public service broadcasters still have to embrace the ethos of individual preferences, even as they try to instil a sense of citizenship. For there are some critics who argue vigorously that in the twenty-first century the very idea of a 'public good' is well past its sell-by date. The liberal political theorist John Keane (1991), for example, would prefer to see a far more pluralistic array of services in the place of unitary broadcasting authorities. And Elizabeth Jacka points out that democracy itself is 'a changing and evolving phenomenon' (2003: 181). Like Keane, she adopts a notion of 'radical democracy' that sees contemporary society defined by difference and rejects any notion of the 'common good': a 'plurality of allegiances' in social life demands 'a plurality of communication media' (183–4). Jacka doesn't pursue what this might mean in practice. But others, such as Geoff Mulgan, a former advisor to Tony Blair, have suggested that instead of public funding going exclusively to a big national broadcaster such as the BBC or CBC or NRK, it might in future be spread more widely across a range of new, smaller-scale noncommercial ventures (Curran and Seaton, 1997: 344–5). And, indeed, the idea of 'top-slicing' the BBC's licence fee for this very purpose was mooted again by several British politicians and lobby groups in 2010.

All these arguments are difficult to resist because they're attractively tolerant and inclusive. But I have tried to suggest throughout this book that public service broadcasters such as the BBC are inherently more pluralistic than either Jacka or Keane, or indeed their counterparts on the free-market Right suggest. So the issue is not whether it's *possible* to have a broadcasting ecology which still attempts to fulfil an important collective agenda, but rather the more philosophically interesting question of whether it's *desirable*. Michael Tracey certainly thinks so. But he is pessimistic about our chances of breathing 'fresh life into the ethic of citizenship' when the prevailing global ideology so loathes the very idea of 'public culture' (Tracey, 1998: 38–9). In Britain, the BBC's official historian Jean Seaton is more upbeat. She points out that, despite all the criticism from Left and Right, there remains 'a resilient consensus' in favour of public service broadcasting (Curran and Seaton, 1997: 319). A 2009 opinion poll showed rising, rather than falling levels of support for the BBC: 77 per cent of those questioned agreed that the BBC is 'an institution to be proud of', up from 68 per cent in 2004. At the same time, audience data showed 98 per cent of the public using at least one BBC service each week (Barnett and Seaton, 2010: 331). Even in America, 2011 figures show about half the country using public media – TV, radio or online – each month. And National Public Radio, while undoubtedly remaining a much more marginal entity than the BBC, has seen its audience climb steadily over the past decade, reaching more than 26 million listeners each week by the end of 2011 (NPR, 2011).

Consumers, then, have been given the chance to express their choice. And, so far at least, they've used that choice to vote rather decisively in favour of keeping public service broadcasting. All of which suggests that, if we leave media theorists or free-marketeers to one side, the concept of public good is still very much alive among that group whose opinions now count the most – the public itself. Indeed, it might be possible to enlist 'consumer sovereignty' in defence of public service broadcasting in one other important way: by arguing that it makes us better consumers. One way in which this happens is through its greater commitment to broadcasting news and discussion, which ensures the free flow of reliable and independent information and thus helps the public to make informed choices (Steemers, 2001: 74). But, more importantly, it happens because public service broadcasting generally embodies a dynamic view of human nature. As Garnham (2000) shows, the key issue is not whether one system encourages 'active' audiences – able to express their own tastes and preferences – and another encourages 'passive' audiences – being offered a pre-determined diet. It is whether these media foster 'reflexive' or 'habitual' behaviours. Thus, Garnham points out, we might actively choose, but in so doing we often habitually opt for 'the non-coercive but active acceptance of domination' (111). A more reflexive process would involve us choosing less intuitively – in other words, after what Kahneman would call a bit of constructive 'slow thinking'. For Garnham, media fail to nurture this reflexive behaviour when, usually for commercial reasons, they offer programming which is 'tailored' in advance 'to the known desires and spending patterns' of audiences, defined as markets. In other words, supposedly 'diverse' programming crystallizes only a limited range of audience tastes and interests out of a much wider potential range: fields of action are closed down, identities repressed. What's made available for consumption and to whom is 'structured – and intentionally structured – in specific, determinate ways' (135). By way of contrast, Garnham suggests, a genuinely *public*-orientated media system is one which makes possible many more 'fields of action' or identities. In this respect, broadcasting needs to be thought of as continuing an 'unfinished' Enlightenment project: to help us become more critical human beings whenever we exercise choice, by constantly exposing us to the clash of varied opinions, the complexity of ideas, the unexpected and provocative perspective.

Now this nurturing of the critical faculties might not always be wanted – except, perhaps, in hindsight. But as Martha Nussbaum and Amartya Sen have argued (1993), a more inspiring view of human nature assumes the pursuit of private interest can be balanced with a sense of deferred gratification, empathy and altruism. It is possible, they suggest, to agree socially on a range of basic needs or, even better, 'capabilities' which the individual consumer might not recognize at first, but which will be of benefit to them and to others. A national system of free education is the classic example of this 'externality'. But, public service broadcasting is arguably one of the most powerful educative forces of the contemporary age. And if so, it's surely reasonable to conclude that it, too, should remain available – even if, at any given moment in time, an audience doesn't demand it.

6 Trust: Public Service in the New Media World

It seems rather strange to talk about public service broadcasting in an age dominated by the Internet, digitalization and social media. For most of this book we have been restricting our discussion to radio and television. With the Internet now so pervasive, and able to carry audio and moving images as well as text, these twin pillars of broadcasting become, by default, 'old media'. Indeed the whole concept of 'broadcasting' – transmitting programmes from a fixed, central point of production outwards to a large and dispersed audience – seems utterly redundant now we've moved into a less hierarchical 'network' age, with information travelling freely in all directions. Treating either radio or television as constituting a self-contained entity seems absurd. Even paired up they now only represent a small part of the overall media landscape. At the very least, we need to stop talking about public service *broadcasting* and start talking about public service *media* or public service *communication*.

But why stop there? The problem's not solved by dispensing with the word 'broadcasting': that phrase 'public service' is also now more questionable than ever. After all, in this new media age some of the arguments advanced in the last chapter – that 'deregulation' in broadcasting during the 1980s and 1990s failed to offer more than a modest increase in genuine choice, or that television and radio should still be treated as social goods because they use a relatively scarce physical resource – are now pretty hard to sustain. When digital technology makes possible a near infinite number of outlets, as John Street reminds us, the net effect is to erode the notion of 'the "public" itself' (2001: 177–8). And when the 'core theology' of broadcasting as a necessary social good is undermined, so too, it is said, are 'the cathedrals built to espouse it' (Tracey, 1998: 17). Who really needs the BBC, or the ABC or the CBC, or any of their counterparts elsewhere, when anyone wanting to hear serious classical music or watch the grainy video of a terrorist atrocity can almost certainly track this stuff down in seconds somewhere on the Internet? Indeed who needs a whole industry of publicly funded professional broadcasters toiling away at pre-selecting material, producing programmes or creating schedules for us, when we can shoot our own films, record our own audio, write our own blogs and listen or watch or share among friends whatever we want whenever we want?

It's not just that as we spend more and more time online fewer and fewer of us might have time left to use the two older media – and that we might then legitimately question the need to carry on paying for them. More fundamentally, it's also that fewer and fewer of us are likely to see any point at all in having other people 'dictate' what we watch and hear. Together, interactivity, combined with the new 'long tail' of services effect a profound shift in how we think about the relationship between the communicator and the audience, and between the 'producer' and the 'consumer'. As we reject the paradigm of broadcasting's unidirectional definition of what is good or true or important, and embrace instead a paradigm of the Internet's apparently non-hierarchical marketplace of ideas and knowledge and stories, divisions of labour are blurred to the point of oblivion. Indeed, in a technologically supercharged egalitarian age, the whole notion of programmes as a kind of 'priestly offering of the host to the congregation' appears utterly archaic (Tracey, 1998: 49). As Clay Shirky, one of the leading enthusiasts of the new media age, argues, those broadcasters or journalists who complain that there's now an abundance of public thought that doesn't come from themselves, are 'keening at a wake': 'The change they are protesting is already in the past' (Brockman, 2011: 6–7). Public service broadcasting – originally conceived as a means of showing us a wider world, and shaping us into more cultivated, more informed, clearer-thinking humans – is losing whatever normative hold it once had.

Shirky doesn't lament this state of affairs, for he points instead to a multitude of *new* sources of information and guidance and values – and, more importantly, to the potential for a new ethos of sharing and participative creativity offered by the online world. In his book *Cognitive Surplus* (2010), he writes, for instance, of a web-based service that helps Kenyans track outbreaks of ethnic violence by pooling dispersed information – something the national government and the professional media had failed to do. 'A handful of people, working with cheap tools and little time or money to spare, managed to carve out enough collective goodwill from the community to create a resource that no one could have imagined even five years ago' (17). Indeed, David Gauntlett suggests, a significant part of the joy – as well as the social value – in this online creativity, as in all 'amateur' craft, is that 'it does *not* rely on hierarchies of experts and elites to be validated, and does not depend on editors and gatekeepers for its circulation': the satisfaction we experience in creating something for ourselves is a measure of just how much we are denied when merely consuming stuff produced by others – or by machines (2011: 218). As Gauntlett puts it, happiness 'flows from action, not passivity'. Like Shirky, therefore, he celebrates a shift – embodied in Web 2.0 interactivity, if not confined to it: from the 'sit back and be told' model of the twentieth century to a 'making and doing' one being revived in the twenty-first (223).

Many of the benefits which follow from the extraordinary plurality of voices and opinions and sources of information to be found online are hard to dispute. Blogs, for example, can offer insights that are uninhibited by editorial guidelines – 'reactive, punchy, conversational, knowing, and free-associative', shaking up our tired notions of what can be said and by whom (Boxer, 2008). In which case blogging is, perhaps, but one small example of a larger trend: what Milad Doueihi (2011) has labelled the 'anthology' ethos of digital culture, whereby disparate pieces of material or ideas or voices are assembled under a loose unifying cover, creating a mode of reading which is comparative and collaborative – representative, in other words, of a new kind of sociability. Other writers draw attention to the value of search engines such as Google in democratizing information. The evolutionary biologist Richard Dawkins, for instance, notes that the Internet is 'suprahumanly large' (Brockman, 2011: 10). It therefore allows him to instantly access and analyze vast amounts of data. More than that, in allowing scientists in different countries to use the same database and communicate their ideas about it with each other in real time, it makes the pooling of knowledge so much easier and faster – extending the sum total of human knowledge through better collaboration. Dawkins implicitly acknowledges what James Surowiecki has labelled 'the wisdom of crowds': the idea that asking lots of people a question is more likely to give us the right answer than following that old habit of chasing 'the expert' (2005: xv). For enthusiasts, all this makes for an exhilarating shift in intellectual life – as big as the Gutenberg revolution of the late fifteenth century with its heady rush of printed books. The Internet doesn't just add to our sum of knowledge, it is said. It makes thought itself more democratic.

Given this democratic feel, we often find that wherever a powerful, vigorous, questioning and inclusive ethos is to be found, new media claim that it is they, not the old media, which have created it. The 'Arab Spring' of 2011, for example, saw young activists in Egypt apparently making good use of Twitter and mobile phones to organize protests, and so help topple from power Hosni Mubarak – while his apologists were still propagating their views on state-controlled television till the bitter end. In Iran in 2009, where grass-roots complaints from opposition figures using Twitter and Facebook about the 'stolen' presidential election reached a global stage – Shirky described it as the 'first revolution ... transformed by social media' (Lehmann, 2011). A similar, if less dramatic vision of crowd-sourced social virtue emerged in the aftermath of urban riots in British cities in 2011. In that case, a single suggestion that Twitter users in just one town might take to the streets to help clear up the damage spread via the popular hashtag #riotcleanup, so that within twenty-four hours more than 12,000 people had posted similar messages, and these, in turn, had been retweeted more than 31,000 times, reaching 7 million users and prompting an extraordinary citizen-inspired clean-up operation across London and the southeast (*Guardian*, 7 December 2011). All these events seemed to confirm that the notion of 'the public' hasn't been disappearing so much as being *re-invented* – as a dynamic bottom-up phenomenon which helps us dispense entirely with the notion that experts or centrally organized institutions are needed for a 'social good' to thrive.

But I want to suggest that public service broadcasting – whether disaggregated into its three constituent words or taken together as a unitary idea – is emphatically *not* redundant. Nor need it be marginalized. True, the word 'broadcasting' itself is a little vulnerable. We probably now need to accept the phrase public service *media* as being more sensible than one which regards radio and television as an exclusive and natural pairing. But even if we accept the inherent multi-media character of contemporary society, with sounds and images melded seamlessly with text on a large range of platforms, we're confronted with the stubborn survival of radio and television well beyond the moment of their predicted demise. Indeed, we need to recognize that new forms of social media sometimes serve old media rather than replace them, and that new symbiotic relationships are even now being forged. One area to be explored, then, is the way broadcasting is adapting to the new media age rather than being overwhelmed by it.

Two other aspects of change demand attention. The first is that, whatever the perceived merits of new or social media, a significant body of opinion worries at the possible downsides they might entail. Even in the 1990s, Michael Tracey suggested that the character of new technologies, offering plentiful, interactive communications, with their emphasis on 'the visual, immediate, and sensual', come at the expense of 'the deliberative and cerebral' (1998: 17). Since then, a plethora of cognitive psychologists, information theorists and social scientists have added their considerable weight to the idea that we should temper our cyber-utopianism. Another area to be explored, then, is that the notion of expertise, or even of centrally organized cultural institutions, might have continuing value as 'filter' or guide. And there is a more radical notion to be aired, too: that organizations such as the BBC might in the end represent the *best* hope of ensuring that the global forums being created by new media are truly democratic and accessible, through helping to develop the notion of a 'digital public space'.

What underlies my argument in each of these three areas – in adaptation, in filtering and in the forging of new forms of communal space – is the notion of *trust*. The philosopher and ethicist Onora O'Neill (2002) has highlighted the continuing significance of trust in governing society. She argues that, while new communication technology should make it easier to 'check out' strangers and institutions, to test credentials or authenticate sources, they 'don't offer adequate, let alone easy, ways of doing so'. In fact, she says, 'new information technologies *dislocate* our ordinary ways of judging one another's claims and deciding where to place our trust'. It's not new media *per se* that will help us, she implies. Nor will it be a fashionable embrace of transparency. Instead, what is needed is a fundamental commitment not to deceive, as well as a reinvigorated ethos of 'questioning and revising'. And it's in creating spaces for the nurturing of this culture of truth and reasoning that public service broadcasters will perhaps find a new sense of purpose for the twenty-first century.

Adaptation

The ways in which 'old' public service media are adapting to the new media age can be revealed if we look at changes in the BBC since the 1990s. For it's clear that in the UK at least the BBC has been among the most influential organizations, not just in embracing new media but in seed-funding and popularizing it. Very often, the commercial sector has reaped the benefits of the risks and investment costs borne by this publicly funded broadcaster. But the BBC's efforts have also ensured that it, too, has emerged in the twenty-first century with a significant profile of its own as a new media player.

The BBC's investment in digital radio broadcasting in the mid-1990s, for example, was a clear example of a supply-led intervention that kick-started a new industry. It was clear at that point that until digital radio sets were made available for sale to the general public, there would be no audience for digital transmissions. And without an audience, there was no incentive for commercial operators to invest their money. The only way out of this fix was for an organization that didn't need an instant 'return', and which had deep pockets of its own, to begin transmitting digitally, even if that meant, in effect, broadcasting to no-one. Moreover, it had to do so for however long it would take for manufacturers to create new radio sets and bring them to the high street, so that, in time, an audience large enough to satisfy commercial demands would emerge (Hendy, 2000b). Although there is now considerable debate within the industry as to whether or not the 'DAB' platform adopted in the 1990s was the best one available, it is certainly hard to dispute the BBC's historic role in stopping digital radio as a whole from being stillborn. Looking beyond the UK, it is those places with a strong public service broadcasting sector – Canada, Germany and Scandinavia in particular – which have been at the forefront of developing digital radio services, while it is those countries dominated by the commercial sector, most obviously the US, which have fallen behind. In any case, the continuing survival of digital radio means the BBC has been able to expand its services in ways that create a modest increase in programme choice and also put the Corporation's vast back catalogue of recorded programmes into the public domain.

A broadly similar process took place in digital television, through the BBC's launch of Freeview in 2002. In this case, too, the commercial sector had failed in an attempt to exploit new technology because of its inability to sustain the inevitable losses that are incurred before demand reaches a break-even point in terms of advertising potential. Before 2002, the commercial operator – originally ONDigital, and later ITV Digital – had struggled to reach a large enough audience. When it collapsed in the face of public apathy, there was a real prospect that the satellite operator BSkyB would gain a de facto monopoly over digital broadcasting. When the BBC then stepped in and relaunched ITV Digital as Freeview, the model shifted: from a pay-TV service to one that was free to view, and which included a larger number of mainstream channels. This proved immediately compelling to many people who had hitherto spurned 'digital switchover'. In a little over a year after its launch, Freeview ensured that digital terrestrial television saw its share of viewing jump from 10.6 to 26.5 per cent (Iosifides, 2005: 61). By 2004, more than 50 per cent of British households had switched to digital television – the passing of an important psychological barrier in terms of future investment. And by the following year, both ITV and

Channel 4 had joined the BBC in supporting Freeview. The BBC's intervention had been critical, then, not just in popularizing the new technology but, even more crucially, in breaking the economically divisive link between digital television and subscription technology. Indeed, it was the commercial sector's inability, or unwillingness, to bear the costs of long-term investment that meant the BBC has since been allocated the lead role within the UK in helping digital switchover. It is a task that stretches the BBC's resources to a dangerous degree. But it certainly makes it hard to portray the public service broadcasting sector as dilatory when it comes to new technology.

The outstanding example of the BBC's catalytic effect in new media, though, has been its move into a large-scale presence on the Internet. Its former Director-General John Birt was instrumental here. Indeed, the television executive Peter Bazalgette has described Birt as 'arguably the BBC's greatest visionary since Lord Reith' principally for his having spotted 'earlier than any other broadcaster' the extraordinary possibilities of the web (*Observer*, 27 October 2002). In the early 1990s Birt cut funding for radio and television programme production across large parts of the organization. This was deeply unpopular. But cutbacks in these two areas allowed for huge investment in online services, the most significant of which was the launch in 1997 of bbc.co.uk. This grew rapidly in terms of scope and complexity, and was enriched from an early stage with embedded audio and video clips as well as numerous links to relevant external sites. It was soon being described internally as the Corporation's 'third medium' (Moe, 2008: 226). By 1996, the site had expanded into a wide-ranging portal – by far the most visited website in Europe, and with a news service commonly regarded as 'among the best and most comprehensible available' (227). Peter Bazalgette even claimed that the BBC had 'led the world with its online news services' (*Observer*, 27 October 2002). Of course, as with digital radio, there are other public service broadcasters, such as NRK in Norway and ARD in Germany, which have also been in the vanguard when it comes to developing online services.

Such confident expansion into new terrain has inevitably provoked opposition. Many in the commercial sector, for instance, worry that organizations such as the BBC are able to use their vast resources to achieve market dominance. They have also drawn attention to various activities, such as the launch of interactive games, logos, school revision sites or ring tones and news services for mobiles, many of which appear to sit awkwardly with public service values (Moe, 2008: 228). In response, the BBC can argue that if it's to retain influence it has a public service obligation to become a global multi-media enterprise (126). A second line of defence is that the BBC's online activities support its alloted role of 'leading the way for the whole of Britain towards the so-called information society' (227). Less often said, perhaps because the BBC is reluctant to appear too belligerent, is that, while commercial rivals inevitably want the BBC's online service to be judged in terms of the degree to which it threatens them – and therefore always wish to see a reduced BBC presence – the real test should surely be the degree to which it serves the public. In this respect, the very size and richness of bbc.co.uk is probably its greatest contribution: the number of pages and links on offer, supported as they are by a global staff committed to principles of accuracy and impartiality, ensures that topics are usually treated in reasonable depth and from multiple perspectives. Thus, for instance, in December 2011, BBC online news coverage of the uprisings against President Bashar al-Assad in Syria, included, in addition to the latest reports from BBC correspondents inside the country, a large number of background features on the President, the rebels and the country, a timeline of events, a guide to 'what you need to know' about Syrian politics and links to external Syrian news agencies, human rights organizations, as well as the BBC Arabic website, with its own extensive resources. Once again, as with digital radio, there's also plentiful empirical evidence of public support for this level of service. Almost 20 million British adults used BBC online each week in 2011 – a figure which represented 57 per cent of all adults online. Overall, the average 'appreciation index' for BBC online was 80 per cent – a respectably high figure almost exactly in line with those for radio and television. Given all this, it's hardly surprising that by 2011, one of the Corporation's six officially stated public purposes (alongside 'sustaining citizenship and civil society', 'promoting education and learning', 'stimulating creativity and cultural excellence', 'representing the UK, its nations, regions and communities' and 'bringing the UK to the world and the world to the UK') was this: 'helping to deliver the benefits of emerging communications technologies and services' (BBC, 2011g: 19). As one commentator suggests, it may well be that in being so prescient and forceful in investing in new media itself, the BBC will 'take its place in the new media ecology through the sheer force of momentum' (Jones, 2009: 205).

So far so good, then, for public service media. But it is one thing to show that an organization like the BBC has retained a high profile. And it is quite another to demonstrate that it is truly embracing the *ethos* of the new media age. For the whole point of new, interactive and social media is not really to provide yet another set of platforms for 'one-way' communication by big institutions, or what David Gauntlett calls 'sit back and be told' media: as he says, it's supposed to be all about 'making and doing'. This is why Bracken and Balfour (2004) talk not of 'public service media' but of 'Public Service Interactivity' and the need for a user-created mandate. It is why Janet Jones wants public service institutions to demonstrate the fact that they are making 'the important philosophical leap from "audiences" to "users" and "consumers" to "producers" – or, to put it bluntly, towards allowing the "user to lead"' (2009: 187). Leaving aside the deeper question of whether there should in fact still be a role for the producer, rather than the user, to lead – something discussed several times already in this book – we need, certainly, to confront the issue of how well an organization such as the BBC is performing against this specific 'interactivity' test. This is a large question – and one that we can probably only answer very tentatively through circumstantial evidence. So I'll offer three examples: the degree to which the BBC is enabling viewers and listeners to create their own 'schedule' of media use; the degree to which it is abandoning a 'proprietorial' attitude to its own programme material and allowing it to be shared and manipulated in ways it doesn't control; and, finally, the degree to which it 'crowd-sources', by drawing on the creative efforts of 'ordinary' people.

First, then, the question of schedules. On the face of it, the ability to create our own schedules flies directly in the face of that old Reithian idea – that we should be offered a carefully mixed schedule which ensures we're exposed to a balanced 'diet' of material: just the right amount of uplift, news, debate and relaxation – a mix we might not be capable of choosing for ourselves given our natural propensity to choose the familiar over the unfamiliar, or the pleasing over the virtuous. Yet, of course, new developments such as podcasts, or the BBC iPlayer, which makes recently aired television and radio programmes available online, have precisely the effect of disrupting any schedules pre-arranged in this Reithian manner: they mean we're free to listen to or watch any programme we want at any time, in any order – and, indeed, on almost any device. In this respect, the BBC's enthusiastic marketing of these two facilities can surely only represent a whole-hearted shift towards allowing the 'user to lead'. The scale of the enterprise certainly indicates that this is more than a token gesture. The iPlayer, which cost £6 million to develop in the run-up to its public launch in 2007, was initially restricted to a limited number of programmes, each available for just seven days after transmission. Since then there have been strenuous efforts to expand the offer: a 'series catch-up' facility, the ability to download and transfer programmes to portable devices, and links to social media websites such as Facebook and Twitter. This last aspect is particularly interesting, since it allows users to 'recommend' or 'share' programmes they like, and to see what their online 'friends' have also recommended. By early 2011, the iPlayer was coping with more than 160 million programme requests each month (BBC, 2011c) – a figure well beyond those for 2007, when some ISPs warned that public demand for BBC programmes delivered online was such that it was placing new strains on the UK's bandwidth infrastructure.

About two-thirds of requests on iPlayer have been for television programmes. And although that still means that more than a million radio programmes are heard through iPlayer each day, it is the podcasting revolution that has probably been more significant for listeners. The BBC began making its radio programmes available as podcasts in 2004 and has done so on a large scale since 2007. By the end of 2011, it was regularly podcasting 320 of its series, and more than 1 billion of its radio programmes had been downloaded; the most popular then being the World Service programme *Global News*, with 89 million downloads. One way of measuring how the BBC compares with its commercial rivals is to see what proportion of the 'Top 10' podcasts on Apple's iTunes are taken up by its own programmes. During one sample week in December 2011 we find that BBC radio programmes occupied, on average, about seven of the ten places. For the Corporation, this represents a 'market share' well above that which it currently enjoys for the two 'old' media.

Since time-shifted 'consumption' is a central feature of both the iPlayer and podcasting, we can make two assumptions: first, that many Britons are evidently satisfied with the ability of the BBC in particular to deliver this feature, and second, that the BBC itself now has a genuinely relaxed attitude to people creating their own viewing and listening schedules. Indeed the iPlayer includes a number of tools that, as it says prominently, 'enable you to find and watch BBC content on *your own terms*'. All this shows the extent to which the BBC now embraces not just the territory but the spirit of the interactive age. Nevertheless, even now, we can detect the survival of several distinctly Reithian ideas. It can be argued, for instance, that the BBC is simply continuing its long-established work of making a full range of programmes universally available – and, indeed, that in marketing the iPlayer so vigorously, the BBC is helping to drive broadband take-up in previously disadvantaged demographic groups or geographical regions. It can also be argued that in detaching individual programmes from their original channels or radio stations, and then rearranging them by, say, genre, the BBC is creating the possibility of new kinds of 'mixed' viewing or listening experiences. For example, the 'music' section of iPlayer places a documentary about the Russian cellist Rostropovich right next to others about Public Enemy, 1960s folk music and Dickensian Christmas carols. So although the BBC is obviously not enforcing a mixed experience for any of its listeners or viewers, it is at least creating the possibility that they can go on an interesting journey into unfamiliar territory should they feel so inclined. This isn't just wishful thinking. Nearly one in three of the people who download a podcast are listening to radio programmes 'they hadn't previously listened to' either online or offline (BBC, 2011d). It is also noticeable that radio programmes such as classic drama or 'highbrow' talk – genres that had once seemed rather ill suited to the distracted background listening characteristic of the analogue radio era – are proving surprisingly popular as podcasts. Indeed, one of Radio 4's most esoteric series, *In Our Time* (1998–), which offers forty-five minutes of discussion by three academics on such matters as Heraclitus, the Etruscans and the Neutrino, was at one stage the most downloaded podcast in Britain. This hints at a rather surprising revival of that old notion of Reithian uplift.

Our second test of the BBC's commitment to interactivity concerns its willingness to become less proprietorial – to be, as it were, more sharing. A changed outlook is certainly indicated by one recent development: the launch in 2011 of the 'Radioplayer' as the regular interface for listening online. The key difference between the standard iPlayer and the new Radioplayer is that the latter doesn't just include BBC Radio programmes: it brings together on one console every licensed radio station in Britain – commercial as well as public. The BBC's former Director-General Mark Thompson pointed out that it 'wasn't necessarily in the BBC's narrow competitive interests' to make it so easy for listeners to 'migrate' to rival channels (Thompson, 2011). But the idea, he claims, is that having a pan-industry online player makes radio as a medium 'greater than the sum of its parts' and so will 'help the industry as a whole'. It's proved harder to achieve this degree of co-operation in television. But by 2011 the BBC was a leading partner in a joint venture with ITV, Channel 4, BT and others – this time for something called 'YouView', which promised a subscription-free Internet-connected TV service. As with the Radioplayer, YouView effectively allows users to switch away from the BBC.

Thompson sees such collaboration as part of a larger vision: ensuring

BBC material will be available in new digital platforms, wherever they open up and whoever controls them. What this means in practice is that the BBC takes a more relaxed attitude to its programmes being copied, remixed, linked to or shared on, say, Facebook, Twitter or YouTube. Similarly, the BBC is now content with people accessing its iPlayer not just through its own online service, but on Freesat, Virgin cable TV, PlayStation and Wii consoles, iPhones, tablets – even by viewers and listeners outside the UK who are unlikely even to be licence-fee payers. The guiding principle, again, is universal accessibility. For Thompson, the sense of direction is now unequivocal: 'All media – sound, picture, text – available on all devices, all the time ... searchable, moveable, shareable' (Thompson, 2006). In other words, the BBC is becoming noticeably less proprietorial about what exactly we do with their programmes.

An intriguing picture also emerges if we turn to the third and final test of public service broadcasters' attitudes to interactivity: their willingness to draw on our own creativity or opinions. One obvious dimension to this is so-called 'user-generated content'. This phrase has come to prominence in the past decade as the increasing ubiquity of mobile phone cameras and free online services for uploading video clips has led to an explosion in the amount of amateur footage of news events. Blurred and shaky scenes of underground passengers scrambling for safety through thick smoke were an abiding visual feature of news coverage of the 2005 London bombings, for instance. Clearly of substandard quality in strictly technical terms, these clips nevertheless provided a raw and immediate form of eye-witnessing that professional camera crews simply couldn't capture for themselves – and newsrooms inside the BBC and elsewhere seized upon them eagerly. It's certainly possible to view this phenomenon sceptically – as little more than the voracious and unthinking use of material that adds a new, slightly voyeuristic flavour to existing bulletins. But a more positive reading is that it represents an early form of what the BBC calls 'news as conversation' (BBC, 2011e). Broadcasting's relationship with its audiences, the BBC admits, has 'changed utterly'. The Corporation's journalists are now told as part of their training that viewers and listeners can 'answer back; criticise; ask questions you didn't think of; add their knowledge and expertise to an evolving story' (BBC, 2011e). One example of this was the use by the BBC and other mainstream news organizations in 2011 of 'user-generated' information during the English riots. In the aftermath, many politicians were quick to claim that new social media played a key role in inciting and even organizing the violence. And it's certainly true that the riots marked a dramatic upsurge in the use of Twitter: in the space of just three days at least 2.6 million tweets in the UK carried riot-related hashtags. Twitter therefore represented a helpful resource for professional journalists: they saw it, first, as 'the quickest and simplest way to post short updates in an atmosphere where using camera equipment ... was risky', and second, as a means of means of gathering more accurate accounts from ordinary residents caught up in the middle of events. Furthermore, such 'citizen-journalists ... collaborated extensively with reporters ... advising on and helping refine the coverage' (*Guardian*, 7 December 2011). In other words, established mainstream media folded aspects of citizen journalism into their own service. In fact, a later analysis of the riot tweets showed that by the end the most 'influential' – that is, those most often mentioned or retweeted – came from mainstream organizations, and principally the BBC. In 2011 as a whole, eleven of the top twenty 'most shared' news stories on Facebook were from the BBC. Furthermore, nearly two-thirds of British adults used social media to discuss the 'old' medium of television. Given all this, we might reasonably conclude that the rhetorical polarity between 'top-down' and 'bottom-up' media – or, indeed, that between 'old' and 'new' – is somewhat misleading.

Yet there is one distinction that can still be made between citizen journalism and public service news coverage: the degree of attention being paid to the ethical and editorial implications of such interactivity. How, for instance, might images or stories submitted via emails or tweets be checked for authenticity? In 2008, the BBC was itself the victim of 'merking' – that is, a concerted effort to hoax a large media organization. Its newsroom was sent an image purporting to show the aftermath of the cyclone in Burma, which it subsequently broadcast in a report for its *Ten O'Clock News*. The image turned out to be one from the Indian Ocean tsunami four years earlier – and the Corporation had to make a prominent on-air apology the following evening. Clearly, no news organization is infallible. But the BBC's on-air apology does at least point to a sense of embarrassment and an institutional concern for getting things right. More importantly, the Corporation now has an elaborate system of checks. It has, for instance, set up a 'Hub', where specialist producers are required to test the authenticity of any incoming user-generated content before it is cleared for use. A checklist involves, among other things, contacting the people who submit an item, and if possible talking to them about the equipment they used and their own location; news agency 'wires' have to be cross-checked to see if there's any image match; data about the number of pixels has to be gathered, to see if a photo matches certain dimensions commonly used on the web; and, finally, an image should be run through picture editing software to check for any signs of computer manipulation. This lengthy procedure is weighed against the usual demands of journalistic urgency. 'Clearly, you do not have to go through the whole of this checklist every time', the BBC tells its reporters. But the balance of advice is clear: 'if in doubt, check' (BBC, 2011f). The 'public service' element here is becoming clearer, then. While including an ever-wider range of ordinary people's experiences and perspectives in its coverage, the BBC can claim that it also retains the necessary degree of critical distance. As a professionalized institution, it has the virtue of being committed to monitoring standards – and, it seems, to the need to continuously reflect upon the editorial issues thrown up by new technology.

Trusting the Information Filters

When we confront the sheer profusion of information and opinion on the Internet the concept of trust moves centre-stage. The ready availability of endless data raises two closely related concerns. First, there's the question of how we test the quality – specifically, the reliability – of information online. Second, there's the question of quantity: how we might control the effects of 'information overload' – that deluge of easily accessed, always on, text, video and audio which seems to characterize early twenty-first century life. Behind these two issues lurks a third: the question of how new technology might also be shaping our own critical faculties. For the science historian George Dyson (2010), the most crucial question is this: 'What if the cost of machines that think is people that don't?'

To begin, then, with the question of information quality. Here, we certainly find widespread anxiety among cultural commentators over the baleful effects of new media. One of the pioneering proponents of this 'declinist' school has been Andrew Keen. In *The Cult of the Amateur* (2007) and *Digital Vertigo* (2012) Keen focuses on the unsourced nature of the information that reaches us. An overreliance on the wisdom of crowds, he suggests, marginalizes and impoverishes those in mainstream news organizations, who, after all, have the expertise needed to discriminate between truth and falsity, good and bad. Without training or editorial quality control, he says, citizen-journalists typically supply superficial observations rather than deep analysis, and shrill opinion rather than considered judgement. Sarah Boxer (2008) raises another concern: the 'survival of the snarkiest'. The snarky tendency that pervades the whole of modern life, she suggests, is amplified by the Internet's peculiar 'attention economy'. She notes that blogs need, above all, to be found – and that being found is a whole lot easier when they are full of sensational rumours, embarrassing videos or outrageous remarks. The result, she claims, is that many have ceased to be useful 'filters for the Web' and become mere 'vents for opinion and self-revelation'.

What gives the opinionated nature of the Internet extra purchase on contemporary culture is a specific feature noted by Viktor Mayer-Schönberger (2011): the sheer *stickiness* of data – whether it is information or *mis*information. Digital technology stores so many details about us, he warns, that we find it harder and harder to leave our past behind, to move on from old disagreements or to remove malicious falsehoods. This is also one of the reasons why the journalist David Aaronovitch (2009) worries about the prevalence of conspiracy theories online. Easily disprovable stories about, say, the 'assassination' of Princess Diana, or the 9/11 attacks in New York being 'secretly' engineered by the Pentagon or Israel, are, Aaronovitch suggests, kept alive by the Internet – sustained by what he calls a 'shadow army' of websites. '"Independent" or "alternative" media sites routinely replicated 9/11 conspiracy material, and many of these sites linked to or cited each other', Aaronovitch points out. Most have consisted of 'cheap movies' made and narrated by non-professional film-makers, 'posted on Google video, YouTube and other sites' – and have typically been 'concocted with the smallest fraction of research' (220–30). In short, the 'information' they offer has been picked at random and shorn of context. Even so, it has all spread at phenomenal speed. The result: a new media age characterized by what Susan Jacoby (2008) calls a rising tide of info-fluff and 'junk thought'.

This brings us to the matter of the sheer quantity of information available. As James Gleick (2011) points out, digital technology has allowed computer memory to increase by a factor of a hundred every decade since the 1960s – creating immense opportunities for research, but also the disorientating effect of swimming in an unending flood of data. Our challenge as humans, Gleick concludes, is to ensure we are still able to create islands of meaning in this sea of information. The question becomes how we navigate our way through this sea and how we then convert the information we find into useful knowledge. In short, our ability to filter becomes more important than ever.

We already have some powerful tools to help us, of course. The search engine Google is now so ubiquitous that it's become a verb. It's also very quick: suggestions appear on screen before you've even finished typing a search term. Obviously, this is easy and wonderfully time-efficient. Might it also be dangerous? Susan Jacoby (2008) and Tara Brabazon (2007) have both pointed to the risk that simple, intuitive surfing gives us answers so quickly that we often avoid digging for long enough to reach a proper understanding of something. For Jacoby, therefore, a Google-powered Internet offers only 'the illusion' of knowledge (2008: xviii). Of course, Google's rise to dominance is based on some innately clever features. To sift through more than 14 billion pages of tagged data it uses a complex algorithm called PageRank, which deploys a vast number of variables. Its specific preference for steering us towards those sites with the most links from other sites is a reasonably good way of reaching the most authoritative sources of information. Yet, no algorithm is entirely neutral. And even with Google we're certainly not dealing with a 'non-hierarchical' media paradigm. As Eli Pariser (2011) shows, its searches are highly personalized. PageRank learns about you – where you are, what you've searched for before, even what you've written about in your emails. Then it gives you the results it thinks are best for you in particular. A different person, in a different part of the world, would get a subtly different set of results. This personalized service is very handy. But, as Pariser points out, it also means we're being directed towards material that reinforces our own particular worldview, ideology and assumptions. The example he gives is a search for proof about climate change: the results for an environmental activist turn out to be different from those for an oil company executive. Since the two sides in this debate are getting different information, we can begin to understand why there's so little meeting of minds: each side is inadvertently indoctrinating itself with its own ideas. Instead of disseminating news and information in a free and pluralistic spirit, then, the Internet might actually cut us off from dissenting opinion and conflicting points of view.

This reverberates through the political system, since as Pariser puts it (2011), 'democracy requires citizens to see things from one another's point of view, but instead we're more and more enclosed in our own bubbles'. In his book *Post-Broadcast Democracy* (2007), Markus Prior offers some fascinating case studies of this process taking place – notably in the US, where he finds steadily rising levels of extreme partisanship. He argues that as the range of media sources expands and fragments, accidental exposure to political debate actually decreases because it becomes easier to avoid; those whose motivation to engage in political debate is already weak start to avoid politics altogether – leaving the public forums to be dominated by those who identify most strongly with their chosen party. This is precisely why the Internet era provides David Goodman with a fitting coda for his study of radio as a 'civic' force in American twentieth-century life. 'Today', Goodman concludes, 'Americans will be getting their public affairs "filtered" in such a way that they will rarely be exposed to disagreeable views' (2011: 181–2). The civic paradigm had always been about creating the possibility of unanticipated encounters, even a little creative irritation. Goodman wonders: has that now gone forever?

The answer isn't necessarily 'yes'. We might, for instance, be a little more forgiving of some contemporary media behaviour. Van Zoonen (2004) suggests that democratic awareness and citizenship can be strengthened not weakened, by mixing politics with entertainment. Then there's Clay Shirky's argument – that abundance will always be better than scarcity (2010: 6). What strikes me, however, is that so many of the critiques of the Internet age we've just surveyed – and so many of those, like Shirky, who embrace the new era as an antidote to the imagined passivity of the television age – come from the US, a country where commercial media dominate and public service broadcasting has been, and continues to be, relatively marginal. One has to ask: how different would their analyses be if their media environment were one with a large and vigorous broadcasting organization committed, institutionally, to nurturing a public sphere infused with the intellectual and creative activity they crave? What underlies their various worries is, above all, the absence of trust: a sense that we cannot be sure we're getting a reasonably open and accurate account of the world. But across large parts of Western Europe, and in the UK and Scandinavia especially, public service broadcasters are large players – and they are still trusted by a large proportion of their publics. In searching for a 'trusted guide' to help us navigate our way through the sea of information in this highly individualized and participatory age we might therefore reassure ourselves that, in the words of the BBC's former Director-General Mark Thompson, some kind of 'Noah's Ark' might be available (Moe, 2008: 227).

A Digital Public Space

What kind of safe haven do we need? It can't be one that turns its back on new media. The Internet, mobile phones, multi-media: they are simply too useful, too enjoyable, too much a part of our lives. And anyway, public service broadcasters are now deeply enmeshed in many of these platforms and embrace much of their sharing, accessible, always-on culture. If we are to discern a new role for older public service institutions, it has to be one that nurtures those features of the Internet that have the greatest potential to enhance civic life.

One example of what this might mean in practical terms comes from Siva Vaidhyanathan (2011). He attributes Google's ascension to being the dominant information portal as resulting from the public sector's failure to act quickly and decisively enough to harvest and nurture these resources for itself. One solution, he suggests, is the belated creation of a vast digital library service, which he labels the 'Human Knowledge Project'. This would represent an alternative to Google's commercialized, data-mined and advertising-directed model by being not just comprehensive, but civic-minded: it would aim to deliver the 'best' information to the maximum number of people, specifically in order to tackle what he sees as the fractured and unequal nature of public discourse. The scope of his ambition is clear: he estimates that the Human Knowledge Project would take at least fifty years to realize. The vision is therefore unashamedly utopian – and, as yet, without any real resources behind it. But Vaidhyanathan's approach is based on the simple principle that universal access to information is too important to be entrusted to an unaccountable private company.

As it happens, an early and smaller-scale version of the Human Knowledge Project is already under way. In Britain, the BBC has recently committed itself to getting online as much as possible of its own vast archive of past television and radio programmes and associated material. This, in itself, is an enormous task, involving more than 400,000 complete television programmes, almost as many radio programmes, more than 6 million photographs, and 10.5 million items of sheet music (Ageh, 2011). One approach to how this might be done was recently tested. The BBC created a beta website called 'Science Explorer', which allowed people accessing details of a science programme to follow links to a range of other relevant programmes in the archives, as well as to any external sites that might be of interest. The very name 'Explorer' has Reithian overtones, of course – conjuring the idea of an organized journey from the familiar to the unfamiliar, an attempt to widen our horizons. And indeed this is how it operated in practice. If, for instance, you caught a radio interview with the biologist John Sulston, broadcast on Radio 4 one morning in November 2011, and then went online to find out more or perhaps listen again, you'd also be offered additional work from Sulston about the 'altruistic approach' to science and about 'progress through collaboration', as well as links to the Wellcome Trust, detailing its research on genetics and disease, various historical resources on Crick's and Watson's work on DNA, and, of course, to several programmes from the BBC's back catalogue about genomes, stem cell research and the relationship between science and capitalism – all of which could then be added to a playlist or 'shared' among friends via social media sites.

Towards the end of 2011 there were signs that such experiments were to be radically extended when plans were unveiled for what the BBC called a 'sort of "Audiopedia"'. The stated aim was to build a website containing links to the entire archive of BBC radio programmes going as far back as the 1940s. Anyone logging on would be able to search the BBC's back catalogue by programme, subject or person. Crucially, they'd also be presented with links to relevant external websites, such as those of the British Museum, the British Library, various art galleries, other collaborating public institutions or even commercial broadcasters. In this way, they could access recordings, images or texts from an expanding range of other collections (*Daily Telegraph*, 3 November 2011).

A key feature of the Audiopedia plan, then, is that the BBC explicitly rejects the idea of creating a 'closed' library focused solely on its own material: it sees the links to other broadcasters' content, as well as to the public museums and galleries, as one of its main features. Because of this, the BBC can present Audiopedia as an example of its collaborative ethos: rather than being proprietorial about content or technical expertise or resources, it shows the BBC seeking to apply its efforts to the development of shared platforms which might both 'help drive economic growth' and help create a public 'space' extending well beyond its own boundaries (BBC Trust, 2011: 12). Indeed, this notion of a public 'space' is increasingly central to the BBC's redefinition of its role in the new media ecology. In recent policy statements, for instance, it has explicitly declared itself 'ready to partner with others to build a shared digital public space' (6). It has also said it wants to create 'a connected, global and continuously available BBC' – with 'universal, unfettered and free access' – across all platforms and devices (14, 28).

This concept of a 'shared digital public space' extends beyond the BBC making its own 'goods' more widely distributed. It is also about finding new, interactive ways of creating national 'conversations'. What this means in practice can be seen if we look at the emerging idea of the BBC as a leading 'Memory Institution' – a concept which involves not just opening up the BBC's archives so that people can watch their favourite old programmes on demand, but also allowing them to *reuse* this material and to actively engage in the debates it provokes. One pioneering example of this approach involved making widely available the archives of BBC news footage of the 1984–5 miners' strike. The strike itself had seen Margaret Thatcher's Conservative government engineering the planned closure of most of Britain's collieries and backing some heavy-handed policing of picket-lines. It had been a long, bitter and often violent dispute – with the media accused of being biased against the strikers in varying degrees. In 2011, the BBC decided to reexamine its own news coverage by working with people directly involved in the strike: former miners, police officers, political activists, local community groups and so on. They were all given direct access to original news footage, and their reactions were recorded in focus groups held around the country. These recordings, which were themselves later added to the BBC's archives, showed people drawing on their own memories to try to redress what they saw as the imbalance of the original reports. As one participant put it, 'personal input' and 'witness accounts' were needed from 'the voice of the people and the opinions of people who were involved' in order to provide context and balance (Ageh, 2011: 6). Others spoke of how the archive material allowed them to introduce children to a lost historical legacy (6). There were even signs that the process prompted some reconciliation. 'Hostility and mistrust were certainly still present', a senior BBC manager admitted, 'but many participants said that after looking through the materials they had a better understanding of the perspectives of others' (7). Overall, he concluded, the trial had shown that, if the BBC were willing to expose its materials to scrutiny and debate, a 'democratic' process might help the inherent public value of private memories to grow and spread.

This seems as good a definition of 'Digital Public Space' as any yet attempted. It is interactive, participatory, democratic. Yet it also attempts to build a universally accessible, transparent and durable entity. It involves a conversation between professional and amateur. It conjures up the notion of a space held 'in trust' for future generations. And although its concerns appear, in this instance, to be uniquely British, it's not hard to imagine the same sort of thing on a global scale. Indeed, in a 2010 speech making the case for an 'American World Service', the President of Columbia University in New York, Lee Bollinger, pointed up how the BBC now represents something of an international brand – and how, outside the UK, it's seen as the template for a way out of the 'crisis in American journalism' and towards a renewed 'public presence in a converged media world'. Why? Because as a large, well-funded, public service broadcaster with established principles, it benefits from levels of trust which, as one new media analyst points out, 'commercial money still struggles to buy or build' (*Guardian*, 26 July 2010).

As for the original pillars of broadcasting, television and radio – they, too, can easily be part of a digital public space. As we have seen, social media and new online technologies are just as likely to revive or enhance our viewing and listening as to displace it. Radio, for instance, is live, mobile, personal: these are qualities which give it 'an intrinsic resilience in the digital environment' (Thompson, 2011). Like television, it is becoming more diffuse, popping up on different platforms as they emerge – it is less obvious, but not less present. And what now gives all media – old or new equally – their public value is an ability to provide a space where information can be converted into genuine knowledge for as many of us as possible. Maryanne Wolf, in her recent analysis of the 'reading brain' (2009), offers us, perhaps, the best model of what's needed – and what, perhaps public service media can potentially offer. The human brain's real brilliance, she says, is that, with all its neural connections, able to switch on and off, to change and grow, it's really a form of 'open architecture': 'we come into the world programmed with the capacity to change what is given to us by nature, so that we can go beyond it' (5). It is an expanding sense of the other that changes who we are. And if we are what we read, hear and see, then public value lies in nurturing within us all a sense of curiosity and an acceptance of complexity. Both act as antidotes to unthinking fanaticism. As will a space to reflect upon what we read, hear or see, without an immediate response being demanded of us: only then can we audit the information deluge. In the end, then, my litmus test for considering any technology is much the same as Sherry Turkle's. In her recent book, *Alone Together* (2011) she rejoices at the ways social media add new dimensions to her life. But, she says, technology is not there for us to like or not like. Our job is simply – and always – this: to shape it to our human purposes. And what could be more public-minded than that?

Conclusion

Barely more than a decade ago, Michael Tracey announced that, whatever its attractions in the past, the era of public service broadcasting was 'probably over' (1998: xvi). With a deep sigh, he confessed that all he could summon up by then was 'a certain dimming of the spirit', since no attempt to espouse its virtues in principle would any longer serve to preserve and protect it: market-based systems were triumphant, digital technology pervasive and he could 'see no circumstances' in which 'the status quo ante bellum' could be restored (xiv–xvi). Writing at much the same time, another passionate supporter of public service broadcasting, Jean Seaton, suggested that the real problem was that the broadcasters had 'been forced onto the defensive' through 'trying to save the achievements of the past'. What was needed, she said, was not an obsession with the status quo ante bellum but to plan 'with imagination for the future' (Curran and Seaton, 1997: 338). While Tracey wrote of public service broadcasting as something that could now only be understood as belonging to the past, Seaton argued that public service broadcasting would only be saved if it broke free from the traditionalist mind-sets of the past and faced forward.

Both perspectives were – and remain – remarkably perceptive in many ways. But they now also present us with two problems. One is that, however well informed were the fears for imminent extinction back in the 1990s, the second decade of the twenty-first century finds public service broadcasting in surprisingly robust form. Not only have traditional public service media – radio and television – survived the arrival of the Internet and social media, they've used digital platforms to reach their audiences in new ways, with impressive numbers of people being drawn to publicly produced material. Some of this speaks to the enduring appeal of the auditory or visual experience, some of it to the enduring appeal of a collective experience or dialogue, or to the successful brand image of a public institution such as the BBC. Much of it, too, is a reaction against the inadequacy of commercial offerings. In America, for instance, the rising audience to NPR's flagship news programmes, *Morning Edition* (1979–) and *All Things Considered*, was put down in 2010 to the simple fact that they, unlike their commercial rivals, supplied 'in-depth reports and stories that can stretch over twenty minutes', and that they, unlike their commercial rivals, featured guests from a moderately wide spectrum of political and cultural life (McKibben, 2010: 44). Though I've pointed repeatedly to the marginal status of the public service sector in American broadcasting, it's worth noting that all four of its television broadcast networks combined only attract twice as large an audience for their evening news programmes. The audience for most NPR programmes, in fact, dwarfs the number of subscribers to, say, the *New York Times*. In opinion polls, meanwhile, public radio is rated as 'the most trusted source of news' in the US (44). To be sure, as one observer of the American scene pointed out, 'success has tended to wash out some of the distinctiveness', and NPR exudes a rather constrained atmosphere of elite and moderate – rather than electrifying – debate (44). Yet there's more to public broadcasting than NPR. Even if we stick to radio, there's the quirky storytelling of Ira Glass's *This American Life*, broadcast regularly from WBEZ in Chicago since 1995 – a show which has regularly covered 'the 330 degrees of life that didn't show up on the newscasts', and which is listened to as a podcast by millions around the world (44). Nowadays, according to one critic, there's a 'small world of heartfelt passionate people trying to do big work' in American public media – encouraged, it seems, by the digital era's ability to let people listen to a programme several times, and the opportunities that presents for less disposable, more layered programme-making, as well as by the programme-makers' new-found ability to reach many more people through new digital 'spaces' such as the Public Radio Exchange (45). This is hardly extinction, nor even mere survival. It's a renaissance.

As for Britain, I noted several times in Chapters 5 and 6 the enduring ratings success of the BBC. It remains a large national presence, as well as a key player in the new media scene. It does so by virtue of public support for its values, its funding and, most crucially, its programmes. Again, as Steven Barnett argues, the BBC's value has, if anything, 'been magnified by the proliferation of channels and new media' since 1998: the uncertainty over income in the commercial sector, the increasing reliance among commercial broadcasters on 'acquired material, repeats and tried-and-tested formats', the scaling back of foreign news coverage by commercial networks, has combined to highlight the need for a well-funded sector ring-fenced from market pressures (Barnett, 2011). When the 'phone-hacking scandal' broke in 2011, revealing how newspapers run by the Murdoch-owned News International had regularly resorted to illegal means to invade people's privacy, the British government was forced to accept at the last minute that News International's parent company might well be unfit to take full control of one of the country's main satellite television companies, BSkyB. The Murdoch papers' behaviour also prompted the Leveson Inquiry, a wide-ranging investigation into the press, which quickly revealed how commercial pressures were driving several privately owned newspapers – and not just those owned by the Murdochs – to abandon ethical standards of behaviour. For a while, at least, the relentless Murdoch campaign against the BBC's market 'dominance' has been silenced, and, in comparison to the squalid behaviour of the privately owned tabloids, the BBC's commitment to ethical standards of truth and public accountability has suddenly seemed rather important. By this time, a group of industry figures had decided that, even though BSkyB now had more revenue, the BBC still had 'infinitely more' cultural influence (*Guardian*, 24 July 2011). And Jean Seaton, who had worried in 1997 about public service broadcasting being 'inhibited' (338), was writing in more hopeful terms about the Corporation as a 'national treasure' (Barnett and Seaton, 2010: 328).

The second problem presented by those earlier critiques concerns the use of history in the defence of public service broadcasting. Tracey had implied that public service broadcasting was now something that belonged only to history; Seaton had implied that its defenders sometimes relied rather too much on history. Throughout this book, I've adopted a slightly different line: that the history of an organization such as the BBC is of crucial significance because, when we strip the concept of public service broadcasting down to those core principles first worked out many decades ago, we find they have continuing relevance to the present. The contemporary resonance of that history applies in two senses here – neither of which is driven by pure nostalgia. First, there's the sense of history which Tony Judt called for in his last major book, *Ill Fares the Land* (2010). Our main task nowadays, he wrote, is 'to remind ourselves of the achievements of the 20th century, along with the likely consequences of a heedless rush to dismantle them': in doing this, we might see that we actually have something to conserve – not for sentimentality's sake, but because it worked rather better than any of its current alternatives (221). Service is often the most neglected part of this inheritance. The very term seems so utterly Victorian, yet its implied message of a pervasive thoughtfulness for others is central – and remains pertinent. It involves imagining us – and then treating us – as individual citizens, not just as consumers to be aggregated and then targeted.

Then, second, there's the sense of history that draws attention to the inherently dynamic quality of certain principles expounded in the past – their ability to adapt to new circumstances and survive in new guises. This, perhaps, has been the running theme of the book, for although public institutions such as the BBC were born out of the very specific political and cultural anxieties of the early twentieth century, the core idea of broadcasting as a tool of Enlightenment is neither static nor time-limited. It bequeaths a powerful emancipatory agenda. And wherever coercive inequality and avoidable ignorance persist, our need for a broadcasting system with an emancipatory ethos – that commitment to fully develop all sides of our humanity – also surely remains.

We must identify what Debra Satz (2010) calls the 'moral limits' of markets – and show why some things should simply not be for sale. There is, as Tracey (1998) points out, a hidden paternalism in market systems, since commercial providers offer what they interpret as the things the public wants. Public service broadcasting is not so very different in this respect. But, being publicly accountable, it does at least remain something we can criticize if we believe it's taken a wrong turn – with a reasonable expectation that our criticisms won't be entirely ignored. It is often out of sync with us – slightly behind the curve at some moments, slightly ahead at others; but rarely is it so for very long, since the necessity of metabolizing public attitudes and then responding organically to this is part of its DNA. Nor has public service broadcasting always assumed it is dealing with a passive population of listeners and viewers, waiting simply to be 'filled up' with culture or knowledge. On the contrary, as Goodman shows, the civic paradigm has been about ensuring people become 'active, responsive, opinionated and individualized' (2011: 76). It is worth reiterating one of the main tenets of Reithian and Arnoldian thinking explored in the very first chapter: the point has always been not to help some people fulfil their potential; it is to make understanding and wisdom prevail.

Public service broadcasting has almost everything going for it except the one thing it needs most: the understanding and support of the political class. In the US, Republicans have campaigned relentlessly against PBS and NPR. In March 2011 they voted to end federal funding of NPR completely and to severely restrict that for PBS. By this stage, true, federal funding only represented a small portion of income for many of NPR's 800 or so affiliates. But the action was punitive. And it certainly symbolized the intellectual failure of elected representatives to acknowledge any public good whatsoever in funding public media. In Britain at much the same time, the Conservative-led government of David

Cameron used the climate of austerity budgeting to hit the BBC's licence fee with a 16 per cent cut in real terms. The licence fee settlement, usually negotiated between the BBC and the government over a period of years, was settled in hours by ministerial diktat. One newspaper report judged this to be 'one of the defining moments in the corporation's 88-year history' (*Guardian*, 19 October 2010). The BBC put on a brave face, claiming the deal at least provided certainty until 2017; naturally, it was obliged to remain politically neutral on the matter. But the disturbing reality is that 2010 marked the moment when the Conservatives' long-held, barely concealed, visceral loathing for the BBC – as a public sector organization with the infuriating habit of being both successful and admired – turned into a serious constitutional assault on its independence.

Once again, politicians complain that an institution such as the BBC 'distorts' the market. But that, of course, is precisely its purpose. The public service broadcasting ethos is precisely this: to transform mere technology into a social philosophy. As Ed Murrow said, when describing the sorry state he felt American television had fallen into at the end of the 1950s, unless broadcasting actually illuminates and inspires, it is 'merely wires and lights in a box' (Tracey, 1998: 16). Much of what appears 'natural' today – the cult of privatization, the assumed efficiency of the market, the disdain for the public realm – is not 'natural' at all. Beneath all this, public values are surprisingly enduring. But we will need to work hard to rediscover them, for without this ambition – the ambition, in short, to have the power and influence to leave the world a better place – public service broadcasting will cease to have any real purpose at all.

References

Archival Sources

All archival sources listed are from the BBC Written Archives Centre, Caversham (BBC WAC).

BBC WAC 1923, S236/3, Burrows Special Collection.
BBC WAC 1929, Letters, 14 June 1928, 23 and 27 July, in RCONT1/910.
BBC WAC 1929a, Letter, 20 August, in RCONT1/910.
BBC WAC 1969, Memo, 6 March, R51/1332/1.
BBC WAC 1970, Minutes, Review Board, 21 January.
BBC WAC 1972, Paper 379, General Advisory Council.
BBC WAC 1974, Memo, 22 October, R51/1147.

Websites, Official and Personal Documents, Speeches, Programmes and Interviews

Ageh, T., 'The Value of Memory', Speech to Prix Italia Conference, 21 September 2011.
Barnett, S., 'Ofcom Review of Public Service Broadcasting: Response to Consultation', 2011, http://stakeholders.ofcom.org.uk/binaries/consultations/psb2_1/responses/barnett.pdf.
BBC 1965, 'The Conscience of the Programme Director: An Address Given by Sir Hugh Greene, Director-General of the BBC, to the International Catholic Association for Radio and Television, Rome, 9 February 1965'.
BBC 2007, *From Seesaw to Wagon Wheel: Safeguarding Impartiality in the 21st Century*, http://news.bbc.co.uk/1/shared/bsp/hi/pdfs/18_06_07impartialitybbc.pdf.
BBC 2010, BBC Editorial Guidelines, 2010, www.bbc.co.uk/guidelines/editorial guidelines/.
BBC 2011, Editorial Guidelines, 2011, www.bbc.co.uk/guidelines/editorial guidelines/.
BBC 2011a, BBC Trust Review of Impartiality and Accuracy of the BBC's Coverage of Science, http://www.bbc.co.uk/bbctrust/assets/files/pdf/our_work/science_impartiality/science_impartiality.pdf.
BBC 2011b, Everyone Has a Story: BBC's Diversity Strategy, 2011–2015, http://www.bbc.co.uk/diversity/strategy/documents.html.
BBC 2011c, BBC iPlayer Monthly Performance Pack, April 2011, http://www.bbc.co.uk/blogs/bbcinternet/img/BBC_iPlayer_performance_monthly_April_FINAL.pdf.

BBC 2011d, 'BBC Radio Celebrates Billionth Download': BBC Media Centre news release, 12 December 2011, http://www.bbc.co.uk/mediacentre/latestnews/121211download.html.

BBC 2011e, BBC College of Journalism Guide on User-generated Content and Social Media, http://www.bbc.co.uk/journalism/skills/production/user-generated-content/.

BBC 2011f, BBC College of Journalism Guide on Hoax Images, http://www.bbc.co.uk/blogs/collegeofjournalism/skills/production/user-generated-content/hoax-ugc-image-checks.shtml.

BBC 2011g, BBC Annual Report and Accounts 2010–11, http://downloads.bbc.co.uk/annualreport/pdf/bbc_trust_2010_11.pdf.

BBC Trust 2011, *Delivering Quality First*, October 2011, http://downloads.bbc.co.uk/aboutthebbc/reports/pdf/dqf_detailedproposals.pdf.

Dyson, G., 'The Edge Annual Question 2010: How Is the Internet Changing the Way You Think?', http://www.edge.org/print/annual.php?aid=how-is-the-internet-changing-the-way-you-think.

Elstein, D., 'What Can We Learn from Mad Men', opendemocracy.net, 14 September 2010, http://www.opendemocracy.net/ourkingdom/david-elstein/what-can-we-learn-from-mad-men.

Fischer, George, interview with author, London, 30 June 2003.

Grist, J., 'The Century before Yesterday: John Grist's BBC and Other Broadcasting Tales, Volume 2' (unpublished memoir, Private Collection, 2004).

Malatia, T., 'Potential Difference: Redesigning Public Radio for a Changing Society', in *Current*, 14 May 2007, http://www.current.org/wp-content/themes/current/archive-site/radio/radio0708vocalo-extended.pdf.

Minow, Newton, 'Television and the Public Interest', speech to the National Association of Broadcasters, Washington DC, 9 May 1961, http://www.americanrhetoric.com/speeches/newtonminow.htm.

NPR 2011, http://www.npr.org/about/aboutnpr/.

O'Neill, O., 'A Question of Trust': BBC Reith Lectures 2002, http://www.bbc.co.uk/radio4/reith2002/.

Thompson, M., Royal Television Society Fleming Memorial Lecture 2006: Creative Future – The BBC Programmes and Content in an On-demand World, 25 April 2006, http://www.bbc.co.uk/pressoffice/speeches/stories/thompson_fleming.shtml.

Thompson, M., Radio Festival Speech, 1 November 2011: full text available at http://www.guardian.co.uk/media/2011/nov/01/mark-thompson-radio-festival-speech.

Secondary Sources

Aaronovitch, D., *Voodoo Histories* (London: Jonathan Cape, 2009).

Amabile, T., 'How to Kill Creativity', *Harvard Business Review* (September–October 1998), pp. 77–87.

Arnold, M., *Culture and Anarchy: An Essay in Political and Social Criticism*, 2nd edn (London: Smith, Elder and Co., 1875).

Avery, T., *Radio Modernism: Literature, Ethics, and the BBC, 1922–1938* (Aldershot: Ashgate, 2006).

Bailey, M., 'Rethinking Public Service Broadcasting: The Historical Limits to Publicness', in R. Butsch, (ed.), *The Media and the Public Sphere* (Basingstoke: Palgrave, 2007), pp. 96–108.

Bailey, M. (ed.), 'Roundtable: Narrating Media History' *Media History* vol. 16 no. 2 (2010), pp. 233–51.

Barnett, S. and Curry, A., *The Battle for the BBC: A British Broadcasting Conspiracy* (London: Aurum Press, 1994).

Barnett, S. and Seaton, J., 'Why the BBC Matters: Memo to the New Parliament about a Unique British Institution', *Political Quarterly* vol. 81 no. 3 (2010).

Barnett, S. and Seymour, E., *A Shrinking Iceberg Travelling South: Changing Trends in British Television* (London: University of Westminster, 1999).

Blumler, J. G. and McQuail, D., *Television in Politics: Its Uses and Influence* (London: Faber and Faber, 1968).

Born, G., *Uncertain Vision: Birt, Dyke and the Reinvention of the BBC* (London: Vintage, 2005).

Boxer, S., 'Blogs', *New York Review of Books*, 14 February 2008.

Brabazon, T., *The University of Google: Education in the (Post) Information Age* (Aldershot: Ashgate, 2007).

Bracken, M. and Balfour, A., 'Public Service Interactivity and the BBC', in D. Tambini and J. Colwing (eds), *From Public Service Broadcasting to Public Service Communications* (London: IPPR, 2004).

Briggs, A., *The History of Broadcasting in the United Kingdom*, 5 vols (Oxford: Oxford University Press, 1995).

Brockman, J. (ed.), *Is the Internet Changing the Way You Think?* (New York: Harper Perennial, 2011).

Brooks, D., *The Social Animal* (London: Random House, 2011).

Burns, T., *The BBC: Public Institution and Private World* (London: Macmillan, 1977).

Camporesi, V., *Mass Culture and National Traditions: The BBC and American Broadcasting 1922–1954* (Fucecchio: European Press Academic Publishing, 2000).

Cantril, H. and Allport, G. W., *The Psychology of Radio* (New York: Harper & Brothers, 1935).

Carey, J., *The Intellectuals and the Masses* (London: Faber and Faber, 1992).

Carney, M., *Stoker* (Pencaedu: Michael Carney, 1999).

Carpenter, H., *The Envy of the World: Fifty Years of the BBC Third Programme and Radio 3* (London: Weidenfeld and Nicolson, 1996).

Chignell, H., *Public Issue Radio: Talk, News and Current Affairs in the Twentieth Century* (Basingstoke: Palgrave, 2011).

Collini, S., *Absent Minds: Intellectuals in Britain* (Oxford: Oxford University Press, 2006).

Collini, S., 'From Robbins to McKinsey', *London Review of Books* vol. 33 no. 16 (25 August 2011), pp. 9–14.

Conolly, L. W., *Bernard Shaw and the BBC* (Toronto: University of Toronto Press, 2009).

Cooke, L., *British Television Drama: A History* (London: BFI, 2003).

Crisell, A., *An Introductory History of British Broadcasting*, 2nd edn (London: Routledge, 2002).

Crisell, A., 'Look with Thine Ears: BBC Radio 4 and Its Significance in a Multi-Media Age', in A. Crisell (ed.), *More than a Music Box: Radio Cultures and Communities in a Multi-Media World* (Oxford: Berghahn, 2004).

Curran, C., *A Seamless Robe: Broadcasting Philosophy and Practice* (London: Collins, 1979).

Curran, J. and Seaton, J., *Power without Responsibility: The Press and Broadcasting in Britain*, 5th edn (London: Routledge, 1997).

Czitrom, D. J., *Media and the American Mind* (Chapel Hill: University of North Carolina Press, 1982).

d'Haenens, L., Steemers, J., Trappel, J., Meier, W. A. and Thomass, B., *Media in Europe Today* (Bristol: Intellect, 2011).

Doueihi, M., *Digital Cultures* (Cambridge, MA: Harvard University Press, 2011).

Douglas, S. J., *Inventing American Broadcasting 1899–1922* (Baltimore, MD: Johns Hopkins University Press, 1987).

Douglas, S. J., *Listening In: Radio and the American Imagination* (New York: Times Books, 1999).

Eagleton, T., *The Idea of Culture* (Oxford: Blackwell, 2000).

Eliot, T. S., *Notes towards a Definition of Culture* (London: 1948).

Ellis, J., 'Channel Four: Innovation in Form and Content?', in M. Hilmes (ed.), *The Television History Book* (London: BFI, 2003).

Fielden, L., *The Natural Bent* (London: Andre Deutsch, 1960).

Frith, S., *The Sociology of Rock* (London: Constable, 1978).

Furedi, F., *Where Have All the Intellectuals Gone?* (London: Continuum, 2006).

Fussell, P., *The Great War and Modern Memory* (Oxford: Oxford University Press, 2000).

Garnham, N., *Emancipation, the Media, and Modernity* (Oxford: Oxford University Press, 2000).

Garratt, G. R. M., *The Early History of Radio: From Faraday to Marconi* (London: IET, 2006).

Gauntlett, D., *Making Is Connecting: The Social Meaning of Creativity, from DIY and Knitting to YouTube and Web 2.0* (Cambridge: Polity Press, 2011).

Gentikow, B., 'Television Use in New Media Environments', in J. Gripsrud and D. Morley (eds), *Relocating Television: Television in the Digital Context* (London: Routledge, 2010).

Gildea, R., *Children of the Revolution: The French, 1799–1914* (London: Allen Lane, 2008).

Gilfillan, D., *Pieces of Sound: German Experimental Radio* (Minneapolis: University of Minnesota Press, 2009).

Gitlin, T., *Inside Prime Time* (Berkeley: University of California Press, 2000).

Gleick, J., *The Information: A History, a Theory, a Flood* (London: Fourth Estate, 2011).

Gombrich, E., *Art and Illusion* (London: Pantheon Books, 1960).

Goodman, D., *Radio's Civic Ambition: American Broadcasting and Democracy in the 1930s* (New York: Oxford University Press, 2011).

Gould, L. L. (ed.), *Watching Television Come of Age: The New York Times Reviews by Jack Gould* (Austin: University of Texas Press, 2002).

Greene, H., *The Third Floor Front: A View of Broadcasting in the Sixties* (London: The Bodley Head, 1969).

Gregory, A., *The Last Great War: British Society and the First World War* (Cambridge: Cambridge University Press, 2008).

Hartman, G., *The Fateful Question of Culture* (New York: Columbia University Press, 1999).

Harvey, S., 'Channel Four and the Redefining of Public Service Broadcasting', in M. Hilmes (ed.), *The Television History Book* (London: BFI, 2003).

Headrick, D. R., *The Invisible Weapon: Telecommunications and International Politics, 1851–1945* (Oxford: Oxford University Press, 1992).

Hendy, D., 'Pop Music Radio in the Public Service: BBC Radio 1 and New Music in the 1990s', *Media, Culture & Society* vol. 22 no. 6 (2000), pp. 743–61.

Hendy, D., *Radio in the Global Age* (Cambridge: Polity Press, 2000a).

Hendy, D., 'A Political Economy of Radio in the Digital Age', *Journal of Radio Studies* vol. 7 no. 1 (2000b), pp. 213–34.

Hendy, D., 'BBC Radio Four and Conflicts over Spoken English in the 1970s', *Media History* vol. 12 no. 3 (2006), pp. 273–89.

Hendy, D., *Life on Air: A History of Radio Four* (Oxford: Oxford University Press, 2007).

Hendy, D., 'Danger in the Air: The Covert Cultures of Early Radio', *Cambridge Literary Review* vol. 2 no. 5 (2011), pp. 121–35.

Hendy, D., 'The Dreadful World of Edwardian Wireless', in T. O'Malley and S. Nicholas (eds), *Social Fears, Moral Panics, and the Media: Historical Perspectives* (London: Routledge, 2013).

Hilmes, M., *Radio Voices: American Broadcasting, 1922–1952* (Minneapolis: University of Minnesota Press, 1997).

Humphreys, P. J., *Mass Media and Media Policy in Western Europe* (Manchester: Manchester University Press, 1996).

Inglis, K. S., *This Is the ABC: Australian Broadcasting Commission, 1932–1983* (Melbourne: Melbourne University Press, 1983).

Iosifides, P., 'Digital Switchover and the Role of the New BBC Services in Digital Television Take-up', *Convergence* vol. 11 no. 3 (2005), pp. 57–74.

Jacka, E., ' "Democracy as Defeat": The Impotence of Arguments for Public Service Broadcasting', *Television and New Media* vol. 4 no. 2 (2003), pp. 177–91.

Jacoby, S., *The Age of American Unreason* (London: Old Street, 2008).

Jay, P., 'Twenty and Thirty and Forty Years On: A Personal Retrospect on Broadcasting Policy since 1967', in T. O'Malley and J. Jones (eds), *The Peacock Committee and UK Broadcasting Policy* (Basingstoke: Palgrave, 2009).

Jones, J., 'PSB 2.0 – UK Broadcasting Policy after Peacock', in T. O'Malley and J. Jones (eds), *The Peacock Committee and UK Broadcasting Policy* (Basingstoke: Palgrave, 2009).

Judt, T., *Ill Fares the Land: A Treatise on Our Present Discontents* (London: Allen Lane, 2010).

Kahn, D., 'Introduction: Histories of Sound Once Removed', in D. Kahn and G. Whitehead (eds), *Wireless Imagination: Sound, Radio, and the Avant-Garde* (Cambridge, MA: MIT Press, 1992), pp. 1–29.

Kahneman, D., *Thinking, Fast and Slow* (London: Allen Lane, 2011).

Keane, J., *The Media and Democracy* (Cambridge: Polity Press, 1991).

Keen, A., *The Cult of the Amateur* (New York: Currency, 2007).

Keen, A., *Digital Vertigo* (London: Constable, 2012).

Khlebnikov, V., *The King of Time*, trans. P. Schmidt, ed. C. Douglas (Cambridge, MA: Harvard University Press, 1985).

Lacey, K., *Feminine Frequencies: Gender, German Radio, and the Public Sphere* (Ann Arbor: University of Michigan Press, 1996).

Ledbetter, J., *Made Possible by ... The Death of Public Broadcasting in the United States* (London and New York: Verso, 1997).

Lehmann, C., 'An Accelerated Grimace: On Cyber-Utopianism', *Nation*, 21 March 2011.

LeMahieu, D. L., *A Culture for Democracy: Mass Communication and the Cultivated Mind in Britain between the Wars* (Oxford: Clarendon Press, 1988).

Lloyd, J., *What the Media Are Doing to Our Politics* (London: Constable, 2004).

Lochte, R. H., 'Invention and Innovation of Early Radio Technology', *Journal of Radio Studies* vol. 7 no. 1 (2000), pp. 93–115.

Long, P., 'The Primary Code: The Meanings of John Peel, Radio and Popular Music Radio', *Radio Journal: International Studies in Broadcast and Audio Media* vol. 4 nos 1–3 (2006), pp. 25–48.

Loviglio, J., *Radio's Intimate Public: Network Broadcasting and Mass-mediated Democracy* (Minneapolis: University of Minnesota Press, 2005).

McIntyre, I., *The Expense of Glory: A Life of John Reith* (London: HarperCollins, 1993).

McKibben, B., 'All Programs Considered', *New York Review of Books*, 11 November 2010.

McKibbin, R., *Classes and Cultures: England 1918–1951* (Oxford: Oxford University Press, 1998).

Marcus, D., 'Public Television and Public Access in the US', in M. Hilmes (ed.), *The Television History Book* (London: BFI, 2003).

Mayer-Schönberger, V., *Delete: The Virtue of Forgetting in the Digital Age* (Princeton, NJ: Princeton University Press, 2011).

Miller, S., *Conversation: A History of a Declining Art* (New Haven, CT: Yale University Press, 2006).

Milne, A., *DG: The Memoirs of a British Broadcaster* (London: Hodder and Stoughton, 1988).

Mitchell, J., 'Lead Us Not into Temptation: American Public Radio in a World of Infinite Possibilities', in M. Hilmes and J. Loviglio (eds), *Radio Reader: Essays in the Cultural History of Radio* (New York: Routledge, 2002).

Moe, H., 'Public Service Media Online? Regulating Public Broadcasters' Services – A Comparative Analysis', *Television and New Media* vol. 9 no. 3 (2008), pp. 220–38.

Moore, L., 'In the Life of "The Wire"', *New York Review of Books*, 14 October 2010.

Mosco, V., *The Political Economy of Communication* (London: Sage, 1996).

Nussbaum, M. and Sen, A., *The Quality of Life* (Oxford: Clarendon Press, 1993).

O'Malley, T., *Closedown: The BBC and Government Broadcasting Policy 1979–92* (London: Pluto Press, 1994).

O'Malley, T., 'Liberalism and Broadcasting Policy from the 1920s to the 1960s', in T. O'Malley and J. Jones (eds), *The Peacock Committee and UK Broadcasting Policy* (Basingstoke: Palgrave, 2009).

Orwell, G., *Facing Unpleasant Facts: Narrative Essays* (Orlando, FL: Harcourt, 2008).

Østergaard, B. S. (ed.), *The Media in Western Europe: The Euromedia Handbook*, 2nd edn (London: Sage, 1997).

Overy, R., *The Morbid Age: Britain between the Wars* (London: Allen Lane, 2009).

Pariser, E., *The Filter Bubble: What the Internet Is Hiding from You* (London: Viking, 2011).

Prior, M., *Post-Broadcast Democracy: How Media Choice Increases Inequality in Political Involvement and Polarizes Elections* (Cambridge: Cambridge University Press, 2007).

Raban, J., 'Icon or Symbol: The Writer and the "Medium"', in P. Lewis (ed.), *Radio Drama* (London: Longman, 1981).

Reith, J. C. W., *Broadcast over Britain* (London: Hodder and Stoughton, 1924).

Rose, J., *The Intellectual Life of the British Working Classes* (New Haven, CT: Yale University Press, 2001).

Rosen, J., 'Making Things More Public: On the Political Responsibility of the Media Intellectual', *Critical Studies in Mass Communication* vol. 11 no. 4 (1994), pp. 363–88.

Ross, C., *Media and the Making of Modern Germany* (Oxford: Oxford University Press, 2008).

Runciman, D., *Political Hypocrisy: The Mask of Power, from Hobbes to Orwell and Beyond* (Princeton, NJ: Princeton University Press, 2008).

Salecl, R., *The Tyranny of Choice* (London: Profile, 2011).

Satz, D., *Why Some Things Should Not Be for Sale: The Moral Limits of Markets* (New York: Oxford University Press, 2010).

Scannell, P., 'The Social Eye of Television, 1946–1955', *Media, Culture & Society* vol. 1 (1979), pp. 97–106.

Scannell, P., 'Public Service Broadcasting: The History of a Concept', in E. Buscombe (ed.), *British Television: A Reader* (Oxford: Oxford University Press, 2000).

Scannell, P., *Media and Communication* (London: Sage, 2007).

Scannell, P. and Cardiff, D., *A Social History of British Broadcasting, Vol. 1, 1922–1939: Serving the Nation* (Oxford: Blackwell, 1991).

Schuchard, R., *The Last Minstrels: Yeats and the Revival of the Bardic Arts* (Oxford: Oxford University Press, 2008).

Searle, G. R., *A New England? Peace and War, 1886–1918* (Oxford: Oxford University Press, 2004).

Sennett, R., *The Fall of Public Man* (London: Faber and Faber, 1977).

Sennett, R., *The Culture of the New Capitalism* (New Haven, CT: Yale University Press, 2006).

Seymour, E. and Barnett, S., *Bringing the World to the UK: Factual International Programming on UK Public Service TV, 2005* (London: 3WE, 2006).

Shirky, C., *Cognitive Surplus: Creativity and Generosity in a Connected Age* (London: Allen Lane, 2010).

Sieveking, L., *The Stuff of Radio* (London: Cassell, 1935).

Smith, Z., *Changing My Mind: Occasional Essays* (London: Hamish Hamilton, 2009).

Squier, S. M., 'Communities of the Air: Introducing the Radio World', in S. M. Squier (ed.), *Communities of the Air: Radio Century, Radio Culture* (Durham, NC: Duke University Press, 2003), pp. 1–35.

Starkey, G. and Crisell, A., *Radio Journalism* (London: Sage, 2009).

Starr, 'Governing in the Age of Fox News', *Atlantic* (January/February 2010), pp. 95–8.

Steemers, J., 'In Search of a Third Way: Balancing Public Purpose and Commerce in German and British Public Service Broadcasting', *Canadian Journal of Communication* vol. 26 no. 1 (2001).

Street, J., *Mass Media, Politics and Democracy* (Basingstoke: Palgrave, 2001).

Street, S., *A Concise History of British Radio 1922–2002* (Tiverton: Kelly Publications, 2002).

Surowiecki, J., *The Wisdom of Crowds* (London: Abacus, 2005).

Thompson, K., *Storytelling in Film and Television* (Cambridge, MA: Harvard University Press, 2003).

Thomson, M., 'Psychology and the "Consciousness of Modernity" in Early Twentieth-century Britain', in M. Daunton and B. Rieger (eds), *Meanings of Modernity: Britain from the Late-Victorian Era to World War II* (London: Berg, 2001).

Tracey, M., *The Decline and Fall of Public Service Broadcasting* (Oxford: Oxford University Press, 1998).

Turkle, S., *Alone Together* (London: Basic Books, 2011).

Tusa, J., 'Implications of Recent Changes at the BBC', *Political Quarterly* vol. 65 no. 1 (January 1994).

Vaidhyanathan, S., *The Googlization of Everything (And Why We Should Worry)* (Berkeley: University of California Press, 2011).

Van Zoonen, L., *Entertaining the Citizen: When Politics and Popular Culture Converge* (New York: Rowman & Littlefield, 2004).

Vipond, M., *Listening In: The First Decade of Canadian Broadcasting, 1922–1932* (Montreal: McGill-Queen's University Press, 1992).

Williams, R., *Culture and Society 1780–1950*, 2nd edn (New York: Columbia University Press, 1987).

Wolf, M., *Proust and the Squid: The Story and Science of the Reading Brain* (Cambridge: Icon Books, 2009).

Wolfe, T., *The New Journalism* (London: Picador, 1975).

Index